ROGER

an extraordinary peace campaigner

by

HELEN STEVEN

The times, writings and sayings of

ROGER GRAY

The Optician of Skye
with a prophetic Insight

First Published 1990

CONTENTS

Page	3		Acknowledgements
	4	Introduction	The Essential Roger
	13	Chapter One	The Far Cuillins
	17	Chapter Two	A Community Man
	26	Chapter Three	A Prophet In His Own Country
	43	Chapter Four	The Courts Of The Church
	61	Chapter Five	A Peaceful Retirement
	76	Chapter Six	A Fighting Finish

The Wild Goose is a Celtic symbol of the Holy Spirit
It serves as the logo of Iona Community Publications

WILD GOOSE PUBLICATIONS
The Publishing Division of The Iona Community

Pearce Institute, 840 Govan Road, GLASGOW G51 3UT
Tel. (041) 445 4561 — Fax. (041) 445 4295

© 1990 The Iona Community ISBN 0 947988 38 6

ACKNOWLEDGEMENTS

No book, even a short one such as this, simply happens without the help and co-operation of many other people. This little book is no exception and I can think of no better way to begin than by thanking people for their help.

Firstly, the Iona Community Publishing Committee, who never let up bullying and chivvying me to apply myself and write the text; in particular Paul Stollard, whom I learned to avoid at meetings if I hadn't done the work!

Eventually, in my moments of panic, it was Ellen Moxley who sat me down with the papers, helped to sort and edit, personally wrote some of the chapters, and then dictated a large part of the book onto tape.

Much useful material, letters, photographs and illuminating stories about Roger's life came from Roger's sister Dorothy Gray, and from his very dear friends Ruth Goodheir, and Bobby and Margaret Harrison.

My scrawled, handwritten notes are largely illegible, and so the whole text was dictated onto tapes and typed onto disc at very short notice and under extreme pressure by Mark Pivac, whose calm competence was so reassuring.

And, finally, my thanks for the inspiration of Roger's life, which I hope may be more widely shared through this small book.

Helen Steven

Peace House, June 1990

INTRODUCTION
THE ESSENTIAL ROGER

My encounter with Roger Gray on Iona in 1979 was typically startling. I had recently been appointed as the Justice and Peace Worker for the Iona Community, an ecumenical Christian community with a commitment to working for peace, and this was the beginning of their annual Community get-together on Iona. Standing on the jetty greeting members as they arrived off the ferry, I was particularly looking for one Roger Gray, whom I had been informed was a veteran peace campaigner whom I must meet. Suddenly a tall, angular, fluffy white-haired figure detached itself from the others, rushed up to me, grabbed my hand and, stammering dreadfully, as excited as a child, told me to follow him and he would show me a wonderful secret. What could it be? No, not some article from the newspaper delved from his rucksack, nor the latest book of campaigning hints in the Abbey library; not some wonderful strategy for action unfolded over a coffee table. I plunged after him for about an hour over the rough heather and bog of Iona, jumping tussocks, plunging through peat hags, climbing down gullies, all at breathless speed to the far south-west cliffs of Iona, there to lie with our chins over the edge spellbound by wheeling fulmars circling their nesting chicks. All Roger's love of life, amazement at creation and deep conviction of God at the centre of all was summed up in that silent wonder of his secret at the cliff's edge.

All the way back we talked animatedly about the madness of nuclear destruction, about our plans for action and proposals to put to the Community, but I had indeed been glad to have been allowed a glimpse of the secret mainspring of Roger's life.

Roger Gray was born in Walthamstow in London on 7th March 1916. Around about 1936 he qualified as an optician, before the required age of 21, and worked at the Refraction Hospital in London. Roger never did anything by half measures, and sometime between 1936 and 1939 he suffered a breakdown from overwork, which left him with a permanent speech impediment.

During the 1939-45 war Roger registered as a conscientious objector and spent the war years working on farms. On returning to optics again after the war, Roger began a drift northwards, working in Edinburgh, and then in Stornoway in the Outer Hebrides. During his time in Edinburgh he holidayed in Skye, enjoying some of the best rock climbing in Britain in the Cuillins, and it was in Portree in Skye that he finally settled and set up his optician's business around 1950. In 1957 he married his wife Mary in Manchester, the start of a deep partnership of love and loyalty.

4

Roger's Christian commitment to peace remained totally unswerving throughout his life. Photographs show him set-faced and determined with Mary steadfastly stepping out at his side marching from London to Aldermaston in the 60s. His dedication remained undiminished and, in their late sixties, Roger and Mary visited the peace camps at Greenham Common and Molesworth. Three months before his death Roger was arrested for the first time in his life at a demonstration at RNAD Coulport where Polaris submarines are based.

Roger's commitment to peacemaking was firmly rooted in an unbounded faith. Although he found himself frequently in a minority position speaking out against the Establishment, there was never any question of the importance he laid on working within the Church. His spiritual inspiration (and often frustration) was the Iona Community which he joined in 1963. He died on Iona while attending the annual Community Week in 1986, and there was somehow an appropriateness about this which reflects the importance of the Community in Roger's life.

Such are some of the facts and dates of Roger Gray's life, but none of these portrays adequately the zestful, inspirational quality of Roger as he was known and loved by so many. This can only come through story and writing. If my own impressions and memories of anecdotes of Roger's life can convey some measure of the man to my readers, then I will be satisfied.

During my astonishing journey to the far cliffs of Iona, it gradually dawned on me that this was not in fact my first encounter. Some years previously I had been holidaying in Skye and while spending a wet day in Portree had been attracted by a most unusual optician's window. This window is amusingly described by Roger's friend Ruth Goodheir later on. Suffice to say that the only reason I could see for the one pair of spectacles discreetly displayed in a corner of the window, was to enable one to read the wide variety of peace literature occupying all the rest of the space. Most intrigued I called into the shop and was shown upstairs into the flat Roger wanted to use as a peace centre. Here I met Roger for the first time, and shared the embarrassment of a man bursting with ideas and enthusiasm, desperately hampered by a terrible stammer. Minutes would elapse while Roger struggled for speech, so that one became almost hesitant to ask a question or promote a discussion because of the difficulty caused.

As I came to know Roger well in later years, I learned to value the courage with which he struggled with his impediment. It would have been so easy to hide behind his stammer in silence, to have relied on the written word, but Roger was a man with a message who would not be silenced. He organized public meetings, engaged in heated debate, served on innumerable committees, and year after year, at considerable personal cost, spoke most eloquently at that most daunting of bodies, the

General Assembly of the Church of Scotland. To do this he practised for weeks in advance on a tape recorder in front of a mirror with Mary as his final arbiter as to whether he had got it right.

I learned also to treasure Roger's words and sayings. Knowing that he might be tripped up by his stammer at any moment, Roger mastered the art of making each word count, and by introducing both humour and poetry into his speeches. Many a time when he did debate, an Iona Community plenary was hushed into bated breath as we waited for a Roger pronouncement and then reduced to hearty laughter by the sharp wit. It was, I think, typical of his humour that, when he telephoned, there would be several minutes of stammering followed by a succinct 'Roger here'!

So many of us are fearful of speaking out for what we believe in; Roger's courage and clarity shamed us to action.

It was as an Iona Community member that I came to know Roger best. The fellowship of the Community and the common commitment to peace as part of the Rule of all Community members were of deep significance in Roger's life. But he never let us off easily, and he had definite and decided ideas as to courses of action, expressed often as frustration when we didn't follow them. He was a great admirer of Michael Foot and Ruth Goodheir describes how the day Michael Foot was elected to the leadership of the Labour Party, Roger in his elation danced a tap dance around her in the streets of Portree saying over and over again, 'Guess who is the leader of the Labour Party?' That the Iona Community did not suddenly join the Labour Party *en masse* was a constant source of irritation and some bewilderment to Roger.

More bewildering still were the Community's wrestling with the complexities of unilateral disarmament. Roger was crystal clear on this and his words are enshrined in the Community's new Peace and Justice commitment ratified in 1988: 'We believe that the use or threatened use of nuclear or other weapons of mass destruction is theologically and morally indefensible and that opposition to their existence is an imperative of the Christian faith.'

Roger's Christian commitment was so clear that he was almost childlike in his amazement that others did not see with his clarity. Ruth's description brings Roger at Iona Community meetings vividly to mind: 'He had a way of jerking his head and shrugging his shoulders as though he was trying to get rid of some invisible burden.' This did not mean, however, that he never listened to opposing opinions. On the contrary, he organized public meetings at which differing views were put forward, one highly successful one being held in Skye with members of Peace Through NATO.

During the early 1980s the whole question of a statement

on nuclear disarmament was high on the agenda of the Church of Scotland for several successive years. The Iona Community would hold briefings and seminars beforehand, especially for members who were commissioners to the Assembly, and for three years running a vigil was arranged outside the Assembly Hall in Edinburgh during the key Church and Nation debate.

The first such vigil in which I participated with the Community was in 1980 and took the form of an all-night vigil, moving from one venue to another situated around the High Street. In one we heard speakers on the faith reasons for disarmament, in another we watched a film, another was an hour of silence, another meditation through song and poetry, finishing with a peace liturgy and shared communion at St. Giles. It was good to move through the quiet streets of Edinburgh from one place to another between stages of the vigil, as much to keep us awake as anything else.

About 6 a.m. we emerged into the Royal Mile with the rising sun gilding the crown of St. Giles and glancing off the windows of the Old Parliament buildings presaging a perfect May morning. All the elation and wonder of a night of prayer and dawning hopefulness for the day's events overflowed in Roger, and he literally skipped up the Royal Mile, jumping off the lamp-posts, indeed it was all we could do to restrain him from ringing the doorbells of the douce Edinburgh citizens!

Later in the day as we stood outside the Assembly singing and praying, it was good to know that Roger was inside on the floor of the Assembly valiantly carrying the cause forward. At one point of the debate he emerged shaking his head sadly and said 'Do you know, they haven't mentioned Jesus Christ once in this debate.'

Roger lived his witness for peace at every level of his life. The following extracts from a talk Roger gave to the Boys' Brigade on the subject of King Hezekiah, shows his concern that young people carry the torch of faith onwards, and gives a vivid insight into Roger's own sources of strength.

This morning we are going to think about King Hezekiah who reigned in Jerusalem about 2,000 years ago. In those far off days the Jews had some good kings and some bad kings and Hezekiah was one of the good ones. In fact he is known as good King Hezekiah, whose prayer God answered.

He was a good king for exactly the same reason that makes people good today. And if we are really going to understand these stories, and if the Bible is really going to mean something to us today we should apply these stories to our own times.

Firstly King Hezekiah was what we call a man of action. That means, a man, or woman, who sees what is wrong and tries to put it right. Almost everyone in the world can see what is wrong, but there are very few people who do anything about putting it right. King Hezekiah acted in three different ways. Firstly he acted in religion, secondly he took social action, thirdly he acted in politics.

When he became king there were all sorts of things wrong with the religion. The Jews were worshipping idols all over the country, and he cleared away these idols and he encouraged them to worship the true God in the Temple at Jerusalem. But he was not just a religious reformer. It is not sufficient just to put right what is wrong in worship at the Temple, or nowadays what is wrong at the church service, it is also necessary to see that people have food and clothing and houses to live in. In those days Jerusalem had no proper water supply, and so Hezekiah became an engineer, and dug a tunnel through solid rock, and brought a good water supply to the city for the first time.

Again exactly the same applies today. It is no use just to talk about God to the people of China and India who are starving because there is not enough food to go around. We must find ways of producing more food and getting it to them.

Thirdly he took political action. In those days, Assyria was a very aggressive nation, and Sennacherib, the King of Assyria told Hezekiah that he would invade his country unless he paid him what he demanded in gold and silver. For a time Hezekiah paid what was demanded and Jerusalem was left in peace, but this could not go on indefinitely, and sooner or later, King Sennacherib invaded the country and besieged Jerusalem. Once again Hezekiah acted. He asked the advice of the great Old Testament prophet Isaiah, who told him to stand firm and Jerusalem would not be conquered. The King took Isaiah's advice and defended the city.

Firstly, then, Hezekiah was a man of action. But that alone does not make a good man. Hitler and Mussolini were men of action, but they were not good men, because they took wrong actions. No, the second and most important reason why Hezekiah was a good king was because he was a man of prayer. I hold that prayer is the powerhouse, one of the ways Christians gain the power and inspiration to do the things in life that need doing.

So many people think that it is only holy and pious sorts of folk that pray, and that it is unnatural. But that is just nonsense. If you believe in God, it is most unnatural NOT to pray.

But what is even more important to remember is that we have to act as well as pray, if our prayers are going to be answered as God wants them to be answered. For instance, King Hezekiah prayed that Jerusalem should have a better water supply, but it did not come by magic. Hezekiah had, as we say, to take his jacket off, roll up his sleeves, and dig the tunnel.

I am going to mention one more kind of prayer, and I often think this is the most important of all, and that is the prayer of thanks. There is simply no limit to the things we have to say thank you for. There is the sun and moon, the sunshine and rain, the sea and rivers, the birds and animals, in fact the whole of Nature. Then there are our parents, our friends, our health and strength.

One of the things I am always thanking God for is that I am alive at this time of history. I think this is a marvellous age and I am grateful just to be alive and able to help in the tremendous jobs that need to be done.

And so this morning we started with King Hezekiah, the good King of the Jews, who lived 2,500 years ago, and we finish with today's Harvest Festival.

But that is what is so wonderful about the Bible. No matter which part you read, you will find that if you study it and really think about it, it has a meaning for us today.

How clearly Roger's immense optimism and faith shines through his words.

Part of peacemaking for Roger and Mary took them on two memorable visits behind the Iron Curtain, to learn about ordinary people in the Soviet Union. If Roger believed in the teaching to love our enemies, then in typical fashion this meant practical action, going and meeting 'the enemy' on their home ground as a fellow human being. As in so many things Roger and Mary were pioneers. While holidays in the USSR are popular and accessible nowadays at that time they were unique. In 1965 theirs was the first British party to visit Rostock since the war, and the tour of the Churches in 1970 was at a time when few people were allowed to visit churches in the Soviet Union officially. To use Mary Gray's words: 'Roger wrote vivid accounts of both our holidays to accompany slide shows which were requested by our friends in Portree, after our return from behind the Iron Curtain, which in those days made us seem like creatures from Outer Space.'

It is often hardest to speak to the people in one's own community but it is obvious that Roger and Mary concentrated in particular in telling their own communities about the Russians as human beings. The following excerpts from a talk given to Portree's Men's Club in 1965 after their Baltic cruise, amply illustrates Roger's capacity for breaking down the barriers of enmity in people's minds, and one hopes that it made a deep impression on the men of Portree.

Each year there are Baltic cruises in Russian ships, which include several days in Russia, but this year, as it is International Co-operation Year of the United Nations, the British Peace Committee chartered a Russian steamer for a peace cruise. As the British Peace Committee is linked through the World Council of Peace with national committees working for peace and world understanding in eighty countries, it was able to arrange visits to East Germany and Poland, as well as Russia, and the receptions we received from the local Peace Committees in the three communist countries was one of the outstanding features of the cruise.

In the second half of the cruise I arranged a chess championship for the passengers and then, having some idea of the standard of individual players, arranged a match with the crew. The three or four of us who were keen on this had some difficulty in persuading the others because Russia is the leading country in the world for chess by a very large margin. But I was very keen on the match, and explained that it would not matter in the least if we did not win a game, and so a match of six boards took place. As expected they won every game and we lost by the rather discouraging score of six points to nil. We had a very jolly hour or two and all agreed we must play again. So as soon as it was convenient for the crew I arranged another match.

Well I do not know whether the Russians were not concentrating so hard in the second match or whether we had improved by practice, but we won one game and drew two others! Mine was a most interesting game and illustrates the Russian temperament at its very best. I made a mistake at the very beginning, but managed to keep alive up to the middle game when my opponent, who had beaten me so decisively in the first match, made a mistake which left us exactly level, with a knight and the same number of pawns each. So despite that I knew nothing of his language I offered him a draw with smiling gestures which were unmistakable, but he, displeased by his mistake, and unwilling to concede anything to an inferior opponent in such an important match said 'No, no.' in a most disapproving manner and concentrated hard on his next move. I sat back completely relaxed knowing that he had not the remotest possibility of winning within the time we had available for the match, unless I made an almost impossibly stupid mistake, and when he realized the position he accepted it at once, shook hands with me, and with the broadest smile indicated that he agreed to a draw. He said 'You are very pleased?', and I said that I was. And so our team was defeated by the perfectly respectable score of four points to two. Our mutual love of chess had pierced the Iron Curtain and soared across the language barrier and one of the reasons I am looking forward already to another trip to Russia is to meet more chess players with as attractive personalities as he had, and who live up to the highest standards of sportsmanship.

On visiting Rostock, Roger's party as he puts it 'disgraced themselves' with their guide, asking to see the inside of a flat in a new housing estate.

As I knew no German I went with the guide's small party and entered a building, climbed a few storeys, and knocked at a door. It was answered by a most homely type of German woman. One did not need to know any German to follow the ensuing conversation before it was translated to us. The guide made his request most politely, and was greeted by a horrified outburst which could be roughly translated: 'Good lord, no, quite impossible', but the guide persisted with increased gentleness and politeness and the embarrassed housewife eventually gave way. Apparently she was saying that some friends had left that morning and that the flat was in an awful state and had neither been dusted or tidied. When we left we were most effusive in our thanks to the kindly lady and no doubt she consoled herself with the thought that she too had made her little sacrifice for the family of man.

And always one to ask the awkward question Roger describes how in a discussion on religious education in schools:

'Our Hosts murmured something about teaching the Bible as literature. That sort of evasion did not suit me, and so, with my usual complete lack of tact, I said "Do you teach school children about God and Jesus?" This outrageous question was duly translated, consternation reigned and there the discussion ended. But at least I had made my witness and the point had been taken.'

The conclusion of his talk sums up Roger's innate hope for the future.

As our cruise chairman, Mr. D. N. Pritt, author and QC said to one of the reception committee, "If the Baltic were filled with all the lies we had been told about the Communist countries we should never have been able to sail up it. And no doubt, they have been told as many lies about us."

But this vast and terrible curtain is beginning to show cracks, and light is beginning to stream through. And if we, the family of man, make the effort, the curtain will one day disintegrate and we shall be astonished to find what realms of light there are on the other side as they will be to discover the light on our side.

Of Roger's constant struggle to bring issues of peace before the Church at both local and national level, and of his passionate outpouring of his ideas on to paper in letters, pamphlets, and speeches we will read more in this book. That which may not emerge in his writings is Roger's deep love of spirituality through silence. He saw his duty to lie in the Church of Scotland, but he often admitted to me that he would really choose to be a Quaker, and Mary made no bones about the fact that she considered herself one.

One particularly memorable week I spent with Roger and Mary on Iona when Father Gerry Hughes led a Peace Retreat for a week. Roger had arranged the whole event and went around the whole week with a kind of secret joy welling up inside him. I still remember our first session on Monday morning when we all sat, pens and notebooks at the ready for fresh insights for peace activists. 'You won't need these', said Gerry Hughes, 'we're going to spend the week praying.' I suppose our faces may have fallen a little, but when I glanced across at Roger he was looking quietly confident.

What followed was a deeply moving week in which through silence, contemplation, and study we explored new depths and heights of spiritual experience. I think of the many weeks I have been on Iona with Roger this was the one which satisfied him most deeply in terms of his faith. Here was a coming together of creative, strengthening, imaginative prayer, and long periods of fruitful silence. Roger repeatedly asked the Iona Community to programme periods of silence into their plenary meetings; indeed he once suggested that the whole of Community Week should be in silence (those who have experienced the Iona Community *en masse* will appreciate the ultimate forlorn hope!).

This book is a collection of Roger's writings, but it cannot and must not be written without warmest appreciation of Mary. In the photographs of Roger on the Aldermaston marches, Mary is always by his side, Mary quietly, gently, smilingly living with and giving strength to a man who must have been an irritation and a challenge to his local community. Roger described himself as outrageous; it was Mary who had to do the shopping the day after Roger's public meetings! Mary gently, firmly going to Greenham Common and walking with Roger to all seven gates on the nine mile perimeter. Mary working with Roger on his speeches, listening, advising, patiently correcting, living on tenterhooks while they were delivered. And when Roger's enthusiastic ebullience exceeded the bounds, Mary's 'now then, Roger' quietly restraining.

One of the features of that memorable Peace Retreat week was a day-long pilgrimage around the island of Iona in complete silence. Sounds, colours, scents were all immediately intensified, every sense alert and open to all the glory of God's bounty. It was a vivid blue-green emerald, blustery day of sunshine and shower, and we saw seven brilliant rainbows during our pilgrimage. Often Roger would say 'Do you remember the day of the rainbows?' I leave the final words of this introduction to Ruth Goodheir.

Roger died on Iona. Mary was at home in Skye. Roger was always in the habit of sending postcards with short messages on them when he was away from home. A card arrived for Mary the day after Roger died. It was a picture of the Molesworth peace camp. It had been raining heavily but it had just stopped. There was a rainbow which seemed to end at the fence. The fence was covered with bright peace pennants. A sudden gleam of sun was picking them out against a very dark sky. The caption read 'Peace at the rainbow's end'.

CHAPTER 1:

THE FAR CUILLINS

In his mid-thirties, London-born Roger Gray came to Edinburgh where his three years working as an optician for Lizars were full indeed. Then, attracted by Gaelic culture and music, he became the assistant optician in Stornoway. He joined the Gaelic choir, walked, cycled, climbed, cut peat, and participated in the wonderful Saturday evening ceilidhs of Duncan Morrison.

When there was no longer a need for an assistant in Stornoway, Roger became the first resident optician in Skye. He championed the cause of Gaelic and the addition of Gaelic street signs to the English ones. He converted a Thames van into a mobile optician's unit and extended his practice to all the southern isles. In the *Optician* he tells of an island visit to a patient living in 'a house in the woods'. Not only was the table ready for Roger and his companion, all the wild birds in the vicinity were made welcome as well — some dining direct from the table!

In Skye, his optician's shop had a window looking onto the main street of Portree. To quote Ruth Goodheir:

Instead of spectacles, as you might expect, this window was full of badges, photographs, etc., all relating to peace issues. One large-framed photograph of which he was very proud was of the Skye CND banner carried through Hyde Park on an Aldermaston march in the 60s. There was a framed statement of the Isle of Skye Peace Centre, a speech by George McLeod, a letter from the Society of Friends, and all the latest peace badges laid out in a careful circular pattern. In one corner lay a very apologetic looking pair of spectacles. When you entered this shop the first thing you saw was a table set with all the latest books and pamphlets about peace. The people of Skye must have thought, 'This is what an optician does — he tries to convert you to CND.'

Indeed, Roger was doubtless largely responsible for drafting (along with nine other opticians) the following *CHARTER* in 1965:

We, the undersigned members of the optical profession, believe that, as part of our service to our patients, the time has come to protest at the possible destruction of humanity by nuclear weapons.

We are increasingly concerned at the continuation of policies which have the effect of perpetuating the nuclear arms race and encouraging the proliferation of countries possessing nuclear weapons, and we declare our belief that weapons of

mass destruction are wholly evil, that their very existence imperils present and future generations, and that there is no faith or principle, political or religious, which could be defended by their use and we call upon our government to renounce the manufacture, possession, use, and even implied threat of all weapons of mass destruction.

We hope that members of our profession throughout the world will join us in signing this statement.

The Isle of Skye Peace Centre was formed ten years after Skye CND began, at a time when CND membership nationally was falling. Roger hoped that through the Peace Centre, awareness would be raised of broader issues — conservation, minority rights, wildlife. Besides the sale of literature, weekend conferences were organized in the Centre. Roger believed strongly in the power of the silent vigil, and many were held in the centre of Portree by the tree planted by Skye CND.

Roger's enthusiasm for the cause of peace was rivalled only by his enthusiasm for the mountains. In *Cuillin Adventure* Roger recalls the events around his conquest of Sgurr Alasdair in 1955. This adventure ended in a disastrous glissade and a fractured thigh. Roger's companion, although also injured, went for help which arrived eight hours later. Roger put those eight hours to good use. During an icy night his first task was to keep his toes moving; then he kept removing his gloves to put his fingers in his mouth, and found great difficulty in putting on the gloves again. He managed to get sweets into his mouth, and most important, to keep his head propped on his hand to avoid sleeping. These necessary tasks accomplished, he was able to enjoy himself! To quote Roger:

It was a fine night, no wind, and was as mild as could be expected considering the ground was freezing. The views were simply superb in all directions. To my left was the gully curving upwards and out of sight. In the other direction I could see the Inaccessible Pinnacle, while straight ahead and below was the corrie, with its small snow-covered lochan, then the moors with the lochan Fhir Bhallaich and beyond that Glenbrittle Bay.

For the first hour or two I watched the sunset. It was a lovely sight as it sank behind a mass of coloured clouds. I dreaded its disappearance, but when it did at last vanish the temperature didn't seem to drop much. Soon the stars began to appear between the clouds, and the sea was bathed in moonlight. It was curious to notice how the further lochan altered with the change of light. As the sea and the distant moors grew darker and darker until I could not distinguish the one from the other, so the snow-covered lochan became brighter as the contrast between it and its surroundings increased. Most of the night I was gazing intently in its direction as it was there I expected first to see the light which would indicate the approach of the rescuers.

Cuillin Ridge — Sgurr Alasdair & Tearlaich from the Dubhs

The advent of the night had however one slight advantage. Until the sun set there were frequent tiny ice falls above me. Apparently some ice fell off the vertical walls, and rolled down the bed of the gulley with a placid tinkling sound. These tiny icefalls did no real harm, but before the cold of the night stopped them, they had covered my rucksack, my loose glove, and nearly all the rope and ice axe. There were two curious phenomena which might have seemed ghostly had I not found the explanation. Some time after my partner had left, but before there was any chance of a search party's arrival, I heard what sounded like a rhythmic beat of axe on ice, apparently coming from below. I looked down, but there was, of course, no-one there. Several times this was repeated, with the same result. Eventually I noticed that it was always followed, at a regular interval, by one of these icefalls, and the sound must have been that of ice pealing off the rocks above. It occurs to me that the footsteps sometimes heard on the hills at night might have had the same kind of explanation, for example, a delayed movement of the ground that had just been passed and compressed.

Then, after about two hours, I saw what seemed like a very faint light, appearing and disappearing, as would be the case if held by someone walking over rough ground, just where I supposed the path by the lochan to be. The light was so faint, as in the case of a star, it could be seen best by looking slightly away from it. But as it remained in exactly the same place, I eventually had to give up hope, and realize that it was not a light but a patch of ice or water which varied in brightness inversely as the density of the clouds in front of the moon.

15

Later on, partly to keep up my spirits, and partly to help keep awake, I started to sing Gaelic songs and hymns. I was amazed to find how much better my voice sounded than usual, possibly owing to the great walls on either side. I do not normally approve of singing or shouting on mountains, believing silence to be one of their greatest attributes, but felt that the occasion was exceptional. In fact, I was so pleased with the feeling of warmth and comradeship it produced, especially the singing of the hymns, that I thought of greeting my rescuers with a song, but at once rejected the idea as they would be bound to think that I was light-headed or that there was nothing the matter with me, and neither theory would bear any relationship to the truth.

And then it happened — the moment for which I had waited and prayed for so long arrived, and I saw, on the far side of the lochan, a light. There was no mistaking this one; it was bright yellow and moving. It would be difficult to exaggerate the wonder, the thrill of seeing that light for which I had been looking so intently and for so many hours, and to know that my efforts had been rewarded, as I was wide awake, still free from pain and apparently unaffected by the exposure. The light seemed to advance quite quickly until the steeper part of the lower corrie was reached, when it disappeared from view for some time, and became visible again in the upper corrie. Meanwhile, other lights had come into view, and it was thrilling and wonderful to watch their flickering progress and realize its significance. It was as though the cold dead mountainside had become warm and alive.

The whole rescue operation was effected with Roger fully aware and deeply grateful. These lines radiate his childlike joy at being rescued so lovingly by his friends and in every little physical comfort which followed. In his preface to *Cuillin Adventure*, Roger enthuses about the care he received at Raigmore Hospital for five **short** months! Once his leg was freed he persuaded the staff to let him sleep outdoors where he revelled in the sunset and the twenty species of bird he spotted!

Wonder and delight in God's world filled Roger's life. He is known to have said that the resurrection from the dead is no more miraculous than the birth of a child, that walking on water is no more miraculous than walking on the earth!

CHAPTER 2:

A COMMUNITY MAN

The commonplace and the miraculous were the same to Roger who welcomed the first first Iona Community Communion shared in the corner of a cafe alive with jazz and dancing teenagers.

And I realized with shattering intensity that the Risen Christ is now, right in the centre of life, the life of teddy boys and the jukebox, life wherever it is and however it is lived. I saw the stark facts that it is not a question of putting Christ back into politics, but of recognizing the fact that he is already there.

I believe that the Risen Christ is right in the middle of nuclear controversy. I believe that it is His will that Britain should cease to be an American base — expendable as and when our new masters decide — and that we should again become Great Britain, our new greatness built on a moral power that not even communism can destroy. Ministers who address nuclear disarmament meetings tell us they are continually heckled by those who ask where the Church is and what it is doing — *and to that they have no answer.*

I believe the Church is the Body of Christ, and as such, should be right in the centre of this controversy; active at all the meetings; prominent in all the protest marches. I believe every Christian man and woman should pray and discuss about this matter in every church hall in Britain. I believe that every adult organization — every men's club and every women's guild should discuss it, and every minister and elder should insist that such discussion and prayer continues until the Will of God becomes known to the whole Church. Then the differences of dogma and tradition that divide the various churches should be forgotten and the churches should come together so that the Will of God might be found for the whole community.

The above is from Roger's talk in Portree on 'Christianity and Polaris'. In the following interview, for the Bible class kit 'Belonging', Roger discusses why he is a member of the Iona Community.

Interviewer: How is that you have come to live in Portree, Mr. Gray?

Roger Gray: I settled in Skye because I prefer the natural life of the village community to the artificial life of the city. It was quite a change coming to live here, after spending my first twenty years in London.

Interviewer: What was your trade?

Roger Gray: I'm an optician. When I found that Skye needed a resident optician I came and started my practice here in Portree. When I arrived I soon found that other communities in the surrounding islands, as well as in the Outer Southern Hebrides and the small Isles of Eigg, Rhum, Muck and Canna, had need for an optician too. So gradually I've developed the practice with the help of my mobile ophthalmic unit. This is a kind of consulting room on wheels, and is very useful indeed.

Interviewer: Why then did you join the Iona Community?

Roger Gray: When I read about the Community and the claim it made that men and women cannot be Christians as individuals, but only by working together, this fired my own thinking. I went to Iona and found that a community did exist and within a few days decided that if it were possible, I'd become a full member.

Interviewer: How does being a member of the Iona Community affect you in your life in Portree and the job you have been doing — being an optician?

Roger Gray: Well, being a Christian is not an easy thing. And it's one thing to be a Christian in a community like the one on Iona. But I'm sure that being a member has helped me, and I've just been thinking that being a member of the Iona Community really affects me in seven ways. I'd like to tell you a little about these particular seven ways.

1. Prayer in daily life.

I try to keep half an hour each day for personal prayer and Bible study. Of course, I often fail! Too often the half an hour is nearer half a minute! But I do not think I would even keep trying were it not that I know that all over the world my fellow members of the Community are trying as well, though possibly failing. While I am not sure if my praying for others helps them, I am quite sure their prayers help me. I can always feel and know some difference on the day of the month that the Community prays for me. I find sins I commit almost every day much less powerful on the day the Community is praying for me!

2. Use of money.

Like all members of the Iona Community I am encouraged to give away at least 10 percent of my disposable income and that is far more than I ever thought of giving before I became a member. I am continually surprised at the joy and help I receive at this economic discipline.

There is also, of course, the joy of those persons or organizations who receive the help and encouragement made possible by our economic discipline.

3 Meeting with other Community members.

Our Family Group, now of three ministers, myself, and our wives, is a great source of help and inspiration. We usually meet in Inverness, and we share our ideas and encourage each other in every way. Although Inverness is over a hundred miles from Portree, we attend meetings in one another's parishes. On one occasion all the ministers came to Portree to help in a public meeting about peace.

4. Use of time in work sponsored by the Church.

Belonging to the Community makes a difference to my work as an elder of the Church. Because of the knowledge and inspiration I gain from Abbey services, and from members of the Community, I am able to offer prayers or give addresses in my local Church or church hall, in a way that would not have been possible otherwise. I find the same help in my pastoral visiting. I also try to bring the same spirit of Community to Bible study groups and other meetings.

In addition to these local duties as an elder, I am able to serve as a commissioner to the General Assembly of the Church of Scotland. There I am encouraged to propose motions on various aspects of international affairs which I have studied. When these motions are seconded and supported by other members of the Community, then the Community draws me into the heart of the witness of the Church.

5. Use of time in local community work.

Perhaps it is in the social and communal activity that life in a village is seen at its best and most resembles the spirit of the Iona Community. Here are six local activities in which I am involved. In each case I am much influenced by my membership of the Iona Community, and in many cases I took no part at all before my association with Iona:

A. Mountain Rescue. This is perhaps the most exciting of our local activities. I am a member of the regular team. We are called out to rescue injured climbers in the Cuillins. This may involve carrying the stretcher down steep rocks, sometimes after midnight. The last rescue I attended was in darkness, except for the torches which we all carried in the wind and rain. The streams were swollen into such rivers that in one moment I was almost up to my neck in water as I helped to carry the stretcher across a stream. The current was such that only a human chain prevented us all being swept away. When we reached Sligachan Hotel at about midnight we were all soaked to the skin. We were given as much food and drink as we could take by the grateful parents of the young girl we had rescued.

B. The Red Cross. There is an active and enthusiastic branch in Portree in which I take part.

C. Civil Defence. We have a Rescue Section and we learn the techniques of various forms of rescue for use in emergencies.

D. Local Politics. There is much political life in Portree. My wife is the secretary of the local Liberal Party, while I am a member of the Labour Party.

E. The Village Council. Here my wife and I, though we are divided on party politics, serve on the same committee.

F. Debating Club. My wife and I are both keen members, and we take part in debating the most important and the most controversial issues of the day.

G. Daily work as an optician. The next effect of membership of the Community is perhaps the least obvious, though nonetheless important. This is the effect on my daily work as an optician. Community membership, with its emphasis on the unity of work and worship - 'to work is to pray' — helps me to see optics in general and my services to each patient in particular as an essential part of my Christian witness.

7. Political Involvement — The Quest for International Peace.

While all the effects are important, and each one is always dependent on the other, I would think that the most important result of my belonging to the Iona Community is my awareness of the absolute necessity of political involvement.

Every devotional half hour I spend; in my economic discipline; every time I meet my friends in the Family Group in Inverness; in my work as an elder, as I pray, or speak, or visit a parishioner; almost every time I examine a patient's eyes; I become more and more deeply convinced that to be a Christian in this nuclear age I have to be involved in international peacemaking. It is necessary to witness actively and effectively at this focal point.

I must confess that keeping alive interest in the Peace Movement is hard and often appears to be hopeless. I know that if I did not belong to the Iona Community I think I might find it impossible. However I do believe that if I am to be true to the spirit of the Iona Community it is in this concern that I have to witness continuously. I am not too good at expressing myself, but I believe that this is really the kernel of the Christian faith. I would only add that I'd hope that perhaps when the young people listening to this interview have had time to think it over, they would at least be able to accept some of the commitments of which I have spoken for themselves.

Interviewer: Thank you very much Mr. Gray. I'm sure what you have said will have stimulated many listeners to ponder and I hope to act.

The vitality of Roger's commitment to his membership of the Iona Community shines out in his paper about the Plenary of 15 June 1985.

For some time I had felt very strongly that there was a basic inconsistency in campaigning passionately for disarmament while at the same time paying for the machinery of the military through my taxes. As an extension to the right of conscientious objection, I wanted to withhold that proportion of my taxes (some 12.5 percent) which was calculated to be spent on defence. However as an employee of the Iona Community, I was taxed at source and had requested the Iona Community, as my employers, to withhold the 12.5 percent. This was one of the main issues for discussions at this plenary, and Roger's determination to support my case, although as will be seen he disagreed with the basis of my decision, is typical of his generous spirit. Such support is a touchstone of community.

I think that the last Plenary was the most mature and valuable I ever attended and, as its primary thrust was the peace issue, a most fitting tribute to our Founder on his 90th birthday. It might be helpful if I comment on the result and suggest at least one possible way of moving forward.

One reason for its maturity, which included reaching a unanimous decision and before the expected time, may have been that we began with a period of Quaker worship. We sometimes feel that we are too busy for as much prayer and meditation as we would wish, not realizing the more busy we are the more prayer and silence we need, if our work is to be completed in the available time.

Another reason for the maturity could have been that the Plenary was preceded by a week on Iona on Christian Obedience and Civil Disobedience.

What particularly excited me was that we came to a unanimous decision despite some of us not agreeing with the principles of the Peace Tax Campaign and, right up to the end of the debate, it was clear that others of us were totally opposed to civil disobedience at this time, and yet, as was made clear during the discussion, we were, in effect, deciding to break the law, for it would indeed be pathetic to undertake a particular action and then, when we are threatened with some kind of reprisal, to draw back and say we do not intend to carry out the action after all.

As I am one of those who do not believe in the campaign perhaps, even at this late stage, I could summarize my reasons for opposing it. They are:

1. Even if we were allowed to withhold the 12 percent of our tax that is used for military purposes, we would still not have prevented our money being used in that way, for the government could take 12 percent of the remainder of our tax and, in addition, it is not possible to withhold other taxes, such as those on petrol or VAT, which all of us, no matter how low our income, pay directly or indirectly.

2. The campaign is based on a desire for conscientious objection. I do not think this is good unless it is unavoidable as, for example, we are told to join the forces or make armaments. I am glad that it is not possible to disassociate ourselves from the arms race, so that we have to work to persuade our whole

21

country to change its policy.

3. If the primary aim of the Peace Tax Campaign is to decide how 12 percent of our tax should be used, this can most usefully be achieved by covenanting 12 percent of our taxable income. This would have the additional advantage of insuring that not only the tax we are withholding but also 12 percent of our taxable income was being used in what we considered the best possible way to achieve the ends we have in view. This could easily be afforded by any Christian for we are considering 12 percent not of our total income, but only of our taxable income.

4. For this campaign to have any real financial affect on the government it would require large support, probably not less than a million, and I think that the time and effort necessary to attain that million could be used in ways more likely to achieve the ends for which we are working.

Despite, and partly because of all the above objections, no member of the Community was more convinced that we should support Helen Stevens's determination to withhold part of her tax and support it to the extent of collectively breaking the law, than I was, as I believe that it is the test of a community's willingness to support activities in which we do not believe, if those engaged in them are clearly more committed and knowledgeable than we are. It is illogical to employ staff to work and sacrifice on our behalf, and then not support them. In this instance we are being asked not to follow Helen's example, but only to support her in activities to which she is already committed.

Before describing one form of action which might enable us, individually and collectively, to move forward, I would comment on what seems to me the seriousness of the present situation. It is said that only those who lived in Germany under the Nazis can understand what is happening in Britain today. I think that is an exaggeration as it seems clear to me that what is happening can be seen in two separate ways.

Firstly, we have already lost our freedom for we are, in effect, occupied by a foreign government – I am reluctant to use the word foreign 'power' as the crux of my thinking is that which we should call evil has no power – that is willing not only to wage a nuclear war which might destroy the whole life on this planet, rather than submit even to pressure from another government, but also to take that devilry and insanity into space where they may eventually destroy other worlds where life may be more advanced than on earth. In the meantime, it is they who will decide if and when we should be annihilated. (Although it is not relevant to the argument, I cannot resist the comment that I never cease to be intrigued by British politicians who support American nuclear arms in Britain, but oppose ours. At least, I would have thought, no enemy would suppose we would be foolish to use our nuclear weapons, but there is no reason to suppose the US Government would not use cruise missiles if they thought, in an 'emergency', that the destruction of Britain was necessary to help them to 'win' a nuclear war.)

The second way in which we seem to be making the same mistake as was made in Germany in the 30s is that we do not realize that we are already past the point at which, if there was to be a widespread rejection of an evil policy, that rejection would have shown itself. Here are two examples:

1. When the Greenham women made it clear that, whatever the cost, they would penetrate the base as far as they could, the Defence Minister, Michael Heseltine, was asked to give an assurance that no such person would be shot, and he said, if my memory is correct, that he would categorically give no such assurance and we, as a nation, were silent. So that if, tomorrow, three, or thirty, or even three hundred women are shot dead, there might be an effective protest from the peace movement, and a few letters to the editor saying that British women should not be shot by British troops, but that would be all. The nation would remain silent, for the magic words 'National Security' now cover any crime.

2. Perhaps not so important, but more spectacular and significant, was the forced removal of a few people growing wheat for the starving, at Molesworth, by an estimated 3,000 police and troops, who separated a chapel, already dedicated by the local Bishop, from those worshipping there twice daily, by barbed wire despite the fact, clearly seen in the aerial photo published in *The Times* the following day, that this piece of ground had no military use whatsoever. According to the June Molesworth bulletin: 'The MOD indicate that they are still considering demolition (of the chapel) and will not allow access because they feel "there is an unacceptable risk that such a concession will be exploited for political ends by those opposed to the development of the base" '.

If the Church in Britain does not rise up as one united body and protest when the government declare that they are prepared not just to close but to demolish churches if there is even the possibility that they will oppose the deployment of nuclear weapons, clearly there is no point at which the Church, as a whole, will ever arise. For now anything – living churches, the lives of innocent women – may be sacrificed on the altar of National Security, a god whom all, including the Church, must worship.

It would be difficult to walk all around the bases at Greenham and Molesworth without realizing that, in some respects, we are already a police state. But Britain is still in many ways a law-abiding democracy, and I am convinced that as long as we have a parliament and free elections the main thrust of the peace movement in general and the community in particular should be to use what democracy and freedom remain, to work for the justice and peace to which, as Christians, we are committed.

The Peace Commitment of the Iona Community, one of the five points in the Rule, was passed unanimously in 1966. Twenty years on there was growing feeling that it should be updated to suit the concerns of the moment, and Roger not only contributed vigorously to its drafting, he actually lived by it. This is it.

We believe:

that the Gospel commands us to seek peace founded on justice and that costly reconciliation is at the heart of the Gospel.

that work for justice, peace, and an equitable society is a matter of extreme urgency.

that God has given us partnership as stewards of creation and that we have responsibility to live in a rightful relationship with the whole of God's creation.

that, handled with integrity, creation can provide for the needs of all, but not for the greed which leads to injustice and inequality, and endangers life on earth.

that everyone should have the quality and dignity of a full life that comes from adequate physical, social, and political opportunities, without the oppression of hunger, injustice, and fear.

that social and political action leading to justice for all people and encouraged by prayer and discussion, is a vital work of the Church at all levels.

that the use or threatened use of nuclear or other weapons of mass destruction is theologically and morally indefensible and that opposition to their existence is an imperative of the Christian faith.

As members and family groups we will:

engage in forms of political witness and action, prayerfully and thoughtfully to promote just and peaceful social, political, and economic structures.

work for a British policy of renunciation of all weapons of mass destruction and for the encouragement of other nations, individually and collectively, to do the same.

work for the establishment of the United Nations Organization as the principle organ of international reconciliation and security in the place of military alliances.

support and promote research and education into non-violent ways of achieving justice, peace, and a sustainable global society.

work for reconciliation within and among nations by international sharing and exchange of experience and people, with particular concern for politically and economically oppressed nations.

In closing this chapter, possibly we could listen again to Ruth Goodheir:

'I think there are some people who act as battery chargers for the rest of us, making us try things and do things.'

Roger was one of these rare beings.

CHAPTER THREE

A PROPHET IN HIS OWN COUNTRY

The local community and church of Portree were profoundly precious to Roger. In island communities such as this it could have been all too easy to marginalize the gangling little Englishman with the peculiar ideas about the Bomb and suspiciously broad attitudes on Christianity, but Roger cared about his community far too deeply to allow himself to be pushed out and threw himself wholeheartedly into serving his community through active membership of his local Church of Scotland and through his dedicated work as an optician. And just as he loved the people of Skye and constantly believed he could make them 'see the light' about disarmament, so the people of Skye came to love him and more than a few may have come to share his vision.

Those of us who knew Roger as the ardent campaigner for nuclear disarmament, may be somewhat surprised to find some of his earliest writings and speeches on Church matters to be on the subject of Church unity. It was precisely his ability to penetrate the fog of debate to the fundamental Christian message that led to his championing both causes.

Roger's deep commitment to the local Christian community embraced the vision of the whole community of the Body of Christ, and his ecumenical fervour is shown in the following two letters to the *Scotsman* and a speech on Church unity to the General Assembly 1972.

From the *Scotsman*, 27 July 1959: 'Celebrating the Reformation'

Sir

The letter of your correspondent, E. D. Strachan, on July 25th, suggesting ways in which we should celebrate the 400th anniversary of the Reformation is both apt and timely.

Although, like Mr. Strachan, I am a member of the Church of Scotland, I consider his letter would have been immeasurably improved by the alteration of two words. If we substitute 'agree with' for 'differ from', the opening of the final paragraph becomes: 'Let us also spread awareness of the points on which we agree with the Roman Catholic Church.'

While it may have been right for the Church to divide four hundred years ago – I express no opinion – can anyone doubt that the time has come for us to unite?

Now we can encircle the earth with satellites, and contact the moon and have discovered forces that make the destruction

of mankind a freely discussed possibility, it is becoming increasingly clear that, as one world, we shall prosper or perish together. We can no longer afford the luxury of worshipping as, where, and how we like and building our traditions and forms of worship into overriding principles.

One has only to turn again to the story of Jesus, consider the emergence of mankind from unimaginable darkness that would have been final had it not been for the Church's witness, and reflect on the wonder and glory of the lives of the saints, ancient and modern, to realize how utterly trivial, by comparison are the differences that divide us.

I am, etc.

Roger Gray

From the *Scotsman*, 3 November 1960: 'No Church to Lead'

Sir

So fantastic are the arguments used by Christians in support of the possible annihilation of mankind, and against the re-formation of the Holy Roman Catholic Church, that it was almost a relief to read your leading article today on Church unity. Within the scope of a letter, I can only briefly indicate why I think your comments are mistaken.

You say the divisions between the various Churches 'are deep and by no means trivial.' The word 'trivial' has meaning only when used comparatively, and compared with what are they not trivial? I suggest that if they are compared with the fundamentals on which all Churches agree, they are virtually non-existent.

You then state that the Churches will not achieve a united testimony by 'trying to impose bishops on Presbyterians and making ministers admit they are second-class priests'. The issue, surely, is whether or not, with the humility demanded of us by Christ when, on the night he was to be betrayed, He washed the feet of all His disciples, we are willing to accept bishops and re-ordination, not because we think it necessary, and certainly not as an imposition, but as a sacrifice to help our brethren in other churches. Then, together, we could re-form our Church which, inspired by our sacrifice, could not only practise – collectively – what it preached, but could lead the nations back to sanity.

To non-Christians who ask why the Church does not lead, and why the witness we should be making is left to a section of the Labour Party, I must hang my head in shame and reply: 'I am sorry, but there is no Church to lead – you see, we can't agree about bishops.'

I am, etc.

Roger Gray

Moderator, Fathers and Brethren: Now that we have seen the report and heard such superb speeches from the four leading speakers, I think it might help the Assembly if, for not more than three minutes, I share with you the quite simple thoughts of an ordinary layman, if only because there are more laymen than ministers in the Church! On some subjects my ideas seem to be unacceptable to most Churchmen, but I think on the question of Church Unity the majority of my fellow Christians share my belief that the union of most of the denominations is long overdue, so that the Church which, we are told, is one in eternity — whatever that may mean — should be seen to be one here and now, and so that our task of reconciliation should be made less difficult.

At various times I have attended services at a dozen branches of the Church, from the colour and majesty of the Russian Orthodox Liturgy to the lovely simplicity of the Quaker Meeting, and including Roman Catholic and Free Presbyterian, in places as far apart as a monastery in Russia and the top of Arthur's Seat on dawn of May morning, when streams of pilgrims may be seen converging on the summit, and in all places and at all times I have felt and believed myself to be a part of the body with which I was worshipping.

But in any event how trifling and unimportant are the things on which we differ compared with the wonder and glory of the faith we have in common, a faith which, if applied, would lead to the transformation of the whole of humanity in a twinkling of an eye. I am reminded of the story of the tramp at an open-air meeting who said: 'We have had Christianity for two thousand years, and look at the state of the world'. The speaker replied: 'We have had water for two million years and look at the state of your face!'

I live on the Isle of Skye, where there is plenty of water and plenty of Christianity, and I would mention just three straws in the wind of the spirit that blows that add to my conviction that the time has come for a bold and imaginative approach to the problems of Church Unity. Firstly, for some years we have had meetings for Bible Study and discussion at the manse, private homes, and on church premises, and these meetings have been attended by our fellow Christians from Roman Catholic to Free Presbyterian. Secondly, a bishop was invited to preach in the Parish Church in Portree, and the only adverse comment that I heard was that his preaching was not quite up to the standards we were used to in Skye! Thirdly, and perhaps most importantly, a few years ago, when our Church was being repaired, the whole congregation worshipped twice a Sunday in the Episcopal Church a few yards away. Sometimes there was a Presbyterian service conducted by our minister, and sometimes an Episcopal service conducted by the visiting canon. My only complaint was that repairs were ever completed! I wished we had saved our money and were still worshipping there, the two congregations completely united.

And so, Fathers and Brethren, I hope that first the Assembly, then the Presbyteries, and then the whole Church will enthusiastically support proposals at least as bold and at least as imaginative as those before us today.

In 1979 Dr. James Matheson became the minister in Portree Parish Church, and a close friendship and understanding grew between the two. During the years of Dr. Matheson's ministry until his retirement in 1984, Roger was afforded much opportunity to promote his concerns for peace. The following extract from a sermon which Roger preached on the last Sunday of the year in 1979 gives some insight into Roger's faith in the potential of his own worshipping Christian community.

Someone once said they were not worried by the parts of the Bible they did not understand. What did bother them was the parts they did understand, and so it is with me. I am not worried by the parts of the Bible I have forgotten or never read, and am not much bothered by the parts of the Bible and Christian teaching I cannot understand. What disturbs me are the parts that are so clear that it is not possible to misunderstand them, such as the Beatitudes and some other parts of the Sermon on the Mount, or the story of the sheep and the goats where Jesus says exactly what will happen to nations who allow the peoples of other nations to starve, for the only way to avoid the challenge of such passages is to pretend that Jesus meant something else or that, for some reason, what he says does not apply to us. Another example of this clarity is the last part of Acts Chapter Two, verses 43-47 where we are given at least nine characteristics of the early Church. We shall find, as we listen carefully to the reading, that: 1. It was a learning Church. 2. It was a Church of fellowship. 3. In the same way that a few ordinary singers can be moulded together into a fine choir, so by meeting and praying together, a few quite ordinary Christians can become a Spirit-filled congregation and church. 3. It was a praying Church. The early Christians knew that they could not cope with hostility of the world around them unless they prayed, and prayed together and, if such a thing is possible, that is even more true today, when we are faced by such massive evils, than it was then. 4. It was a reverent Church. I particularly like the expression 'a sense of awe was everywhere'. 5. It was a Church where things happen, for there were marvels, translated 'miracles' in at least one translation, and other signs of the Spirit. 6. It was a sharing Church, for they would sell their property and possessions and share their wealth among their fellow members. 7. It was a worshipping Church. They did not go to church once, or even twice a week, but every day. 8. It was a happy Church and, finally it was a Church of people whom others could not help liking.

All this and more is in the final six verses of this chapter and our sermon for today. And we will find if we study them carefully that with the possible exception of the sharing ALL our property and ALL our possessions with one another, every part of this section not only could but would apply to us if together we are prepared to accept the Holy Spirit in all its fullness.

I believe that during the past few years we have been led by our minister and guided by the Spirit in such a way and by such an extent that if now, as a church and a congregation, we meet together in all the ways described in these verses, and open our hearts to one another and to the full power of the Holy Spirit, then we will become a community of believers which has all the signs of the believers that are described in the last few verses of this chapter.

Nevertheless, the relationship with his congregation cannot always have been an easy one, as Ruth Goodheir's description illustrates.

One vigil that I won't forget in a hurry was the one we held on the evening of the day that cruise missiles arrived at Greenham Common. The women's peace camp had been in existence for two years and such a powerful feeling arose among our members that we should do something to show our anger and determination to oppose cruise missiles that Roger suggested that we ask for the use of the Church of Scotland in Portree for a vigil. We had at that point about five elders in our group and we went to see our minister but we were refused the use of the church. We then decided to hold the vigil outside the church on Sunday evening. Skye people are strong Sabbatarians. The vigil began quietly and prayerfully enough. We lit candles and sang, quite a few people coming out of the evening service joined us. After an hour or so disaster struck. A theatre group from Edinburgh who were staying in Portree saw our posters and decided to join us. But they decided to show their support by bringing drums and trumpets and making as much noise as possible. I remember standing frozen in horror as they did a kind of snake dance all around us. The church people who had joined us disappeared in all directions. Roger said 'We will have to stop them'. When I explained about the Sabbath they were very apologetic, but the damage was done. There were people in Portree who didn't speak to me for six months afterwards. They thought we had done it deliberately. Just one of the difficulties campaigning in a small community!

In 1978 Roger was sent as a Commissioner to the General Assembly of the Church of Scotland for the ninth time. I suppose that by this time the Portree congregation knew full well what they were doing by sending Roger, as he had spoken publicly on questions on almost every previous occasion. What follows is Roger's report-back on the Assembly to the Portree congregation at the evening service on 11 June 1978, surely one of the most unusual reports the congregation had ever heard.

When Dr. Matheson asked whether I would speak to you about the General Assembly, I said I would not wish to add anything to the general reporting of the Assembly as I thought that had already been done more than adequately by the press and radio and by Dr. Matheson himself the Sunday before last, but I would be pleased to concentrate on one particular debate and describe the events that led up to it, as I think it is valuable, and may be interesting for congregations to know the sort of preparations that are made for major debates such as the one this year on the nuclear deterrent. I should like also, as part of the same process, to say something about the all-night vigil for world justice and peace which was held from 11 p.m. Saturday night. It is sometimes said of the Edinburgh Festival that the fringe events are more important than the festival itself and some might think that the same could be said of the General Assembly.

To begin at the beginning for the story of even one debate one would have go back to Adam and Eve or, in this case, at least to Cain and Abel but, for this evening's purposes, I shall go back just twenty years to the founding of the Campaign for Nuclear Disarmament. I am sure that history will decide, if it has not already decided, that CND was one of the great prophetic movements of this century and even if it had no affect at all on world politics it would have justified its existence by the marvellous experiences of tens of thousands of people on the early Aldermaston Marches. The Church as a whole opposed our belief on unilateral disarmament as it has always opposed prophetic movements in the past, but the last year has seen a tremendous advance in the world-wide movements for peace. The pacifist movement called 'mobilization for survival' began in America and has spread to this country. At the same time, at a lesser level, there was such demand for the Christian CND pamphlet that within weeks of publication a second edition of 5,000 copies was printed.

As part of this world-wide movement the Iona Community, urged on by its founder George MacLeod, printed and posted to every minister of the Church of Scotland a leaflet urging them to support unilateral disarmament now. The replies were so encouraging that we printed a second leaflet giving the names of over three hundred Church of Scotland ministers who had signed the following declaration: 'I support unilateral nuclear disarmament now as the only expression of Christian witness now consonant with the Gospel in a nuclear age'. We put copies of this leaflet in the boxes of all the Commissioners to the

Assembly. And finally, believing action without prayer is as foolish as prayer without action, we arranged an all-night vigil to be held during the Assembly from 11 p.m. Saturday night to 8 a.m. Sunday morning, and to this we gave a written invitation to every member of the Assembly.

Previous all-night vigils have taken place in St. Giles and have been purely for prayer and meditation, with different people leading each half hour throughout the night. While I think their importance can hardly be exaggerated, attendance has usually been very low, dropping to four, three, or even two during the early hours of the morning. The one this year was different in every respect. It began with three services in separate Churches – Roman Catholic, Episcopalian and Church of Scotland – and at midnight we all met in the Highland Tollbooth Church hall for a cup of coffee. This was followed by a talk and discussion on 'Disarmament and Development' in the Church upstairs and this led straight into a service led by Graeme Brown, the leader of the Iona Community.

The time was now 2.15 a.m. and we returned to the hall for another cup of coffee and to see a film. The film seemed to be a kind of documentary about the young men in America who have actually to fire the nuclear missiles and I found it far more terrifying than the banned TV film *The War Game* which I saw some years ago. It was its normality that was so terrifying. Near the beginning the commentator used the expression 'pressing the button' and the young man to whom he was speaking explained, in complete seriousness, as though it were a matter of real importance, that you do not press a button, you turn a key. So now we know. If we want to destroy the human race, we do not press a button, we turn a key, and we were shown a picture of the lock and of the key which turns it. Later a young wife, whose difference from any young wife in Portree was that she spoke with an American accent, was asked if she was worried by the thought that her husband might cause the destruction of all his fellow countrymen and she said no. She understood that if that happened he would be doing his Christian patriotic duty.

After the film we walked to the hall of the Old St. Paul's Episcopal Church where there was a talk and discussion led by an officer of the United Nations Association. I caused alarm and despondency by pointing out that what we had seen in the film was happening in our own Holy Loch and had a fast and furious argument with the speaker. Tired and depressed we went upstairs to the Episcopal Church and there we had what was, to me, one of the three most outstanding and inspiring experiences of the night.

Arriving in the dark and silent and empty Church we left behind politics and world affairs and led by the Rector,

Richard Holloway, whose gentle manner and quiet voice is well-known on radio and TV, we meditated on the sufferings and triumph of Christ as we watched a slide presentation of the Stations of the Cross. Some slides were contemporary, of black and white men suffering, while others were taken from the Oberammergau Passion Play. This was followed by about twenty minutes of silence in the quiet and almost completely dark Church. To Protestants, unused to the wonder of this kind of Catholic liturgy, this was a great experience, accentuated by the fact that it took place at four in the morning when we were passing through what was, physically and mentally, the most difficult part of the night.

By now dawn was breaking as we walked to the Roman Catholic St. Mary's Church. After another cup of coffee, this time with a biscuit, about thirty of us took part in a group discussion led by two young priests. We then walked to the nearby Roman Catholic Church where there was a service at 6 a.m. This again was a real treat for Protestants unused to Catholic forms of worship. The very walls of this great and beautiful church seemed impregnated with the spirit of worship and enclosed the little band of believers with a silence which could be felt. The service was simple and informal and we all joined in the reading of the Psalms and the prayers and responses.

We then walked to St. Giles for the final act of worship, preceded by half an hour of silence. We must have looked a pathetic band of pilgrims. We had had no meal for nine or ten hours and, as the heat of the previous day was now spent, we were cold as well as tired and hungry, and as we tried to keep awake even we were unable to pray or meditate.

At 7.30 a.m. Rev. Gilleasbuig MacMillan, whom you probably remember, arrived, looking very fresh and fit, and led the most truly ecumenical service I have ever attended. We sang two hymns unaccompanied and made a loud, if not particularly tuneful noise. The lessons were read by two girls, one Roman Catholic and the other Episcopalian, and Bishop Leslie Newbiggin preached a most carefully prepared and brilliant sermon on the economics of world poverty and what we could do about it. I thought that address, given to that congregation of which it could, without exaggeration, be said that a third were asleep trying to awake, a third awake trying to sleep, and the remainder were asleep, was more valuable than the one he gave later in the week to a packed Assembly. Perhaps the loveliest and most moving experience during the whole night was the last few moments of the service when, in that great, Protestant Cathedral, a young Roman Catholic priest who had been with us all night and who was sitting with us in the congregation, quietly walked forward, gently led us in a simple and beautiful prayer, and pronounced the benediction on the whole night's vigil.

The time was now 8 a.m. and we returned to the Episcopal Church hall for tea and coffee and rolls. I would think that about fifty people attended part of the night, and about twenty about the whole night through. My friend with whom I was staying and myself had a mile to walk to his home, and we enjoyed the walk across the Edinburgh Meadows on that glorious summer morning under an avenue of cherry trees heavy with their lovely pink blossoms.

Instead of sleeping for the next twenty-four hours, as I had expected, I had breakfast and a bath and after a short rest attended a Quaker Meeting. Rarely has the silence of a Quaker Meeting seemed so wonderful. For the first time on my many visits to the Edinburgh Meeting I spoke during the silence to ask for the prayers of the Meeting for the motion on nuclear disarmament to be moved at the Assembly the following day. What I said arose naturally from the contribution of the previous speaker and led, equally naturally, into that of the next speaker.

All I have described so far was a preparation for future Church and Nation day on the Monday. The day began with Holy Communion, celebrated in the Assembly Hall itself. In the last few minutes I have said much in favour of Catholic forms of liturgy. It is a pleasure now to be able to report that in this celebration we experienced the majesty of Presbyterian liturgy at its very best. There was one quite marvellous moment when, as the roof was being lifted by the superb and unaccompanied singing of the Psalm, dozens of elders emerged from all directions bearing dozens of plates of bread and chalices of wine, marching upright and well-disciplined, as though they realized that they were bringing priceless gifts to their king. The first item of business was a speech by the Prime Minister and this was followed by the report of the Committee on Church and Nation. To everyone's surprise we disposed of the first three sections of the deliverance, including the one on Scottish interests, with hardly a word spoken, and in a matter of minutes arrived at the debate on nuclear disarmament. This was quite different from the many previous debates on the subject when light-weight people like myself who have no influence on the Assembly, moved motions which were often ignored by the media, and were always heavily defeated. On this day no less than three ex-Moderators spoke in favour of the motion: 'The General Assembly, recognizing that the United Nations' Special Session on Disarmament offers the opportunity for a new peace initiative, call upon the Church to urge upon Her Majesty's Government unilateral disarmament now.'

The speeches of the three ex-Moderators were as different as could be imagined. Dr. George Reid spoke with great passion and was particularly eloquent on the subject of the neutron bomb which he described as the 'beautiful new weapon which only destroys people'; Lord MacLeod gave us another glimpse of his prophetic vision and, at the age of over 80, was as incisive and inspiring as ever; while Dr. Matheson's speech was one of the finest I have heard at that or any other Assembly. Not only did he combine prophecy with Statesmanship, basing both on simple easily understood logic, but as he spoke the goodness and power of the Holy Spirit was so manifest that it will ever remain a mystery how any person present could doubt that the Holy Spirit was speaking through the mouths of George Reid, George MacLeod and James Matheson as surely and as clearly as the Spirit spoke through the mouth of Peter at the first Pentecost.

It is with some embarrassment that I comment equally briefly on the two principal speakers on the other side. An elder seemed to base his speech on the assumption that the leaders of the USSR want to occupy Western Europe and invade Britain, and an ex-Moderator tried to mock and ridicule Lord MacLeod in a way which alone might have been sufficient to turn the whole Assembly against him. As the world knows the motion was defeated and the Assembly voted to support the retention of the nuclear deterrent and against unilateral disarmament.

This story has a short and perhaps unimportant epilogue but I should mention it as it concerns myself — and a Commissioner should report his activities to his presbytery and his congregation so that they may, if they wish, make sure that he does not represent them again. On the following day, Tuesday, the vigil seemed to produce its maximum affect on me and while I was on my knees praying in the morning I could almost see a Commissioner rise from his seat and oppose a deliverance of the report of the Iona Community, the last item of the Assembly for that day. And I was certain if that happened I must speak without notes or previous preparation.

After a long session, without the usual break for tea, the Assembly reached, at about 6.30 p.m., the last item of the day and, as a tired Assembly was ready to go home, a Commissioner rose and, for no apparent reason, moved that we change just one word of a deliverance so that we should 'note' instead of 'welcome' the initiative taken by the Iona Community to promote concern for disarmament and peace through its campaign for Mobilization for Survival. As though in a dream I went to the rostrum without a note in my hand and not knowing what I was going to say but knowing I would speak fluently and hold the attention of the Assembly for as long as necessary, I told them a little of the results our initiative had already had and told them about the all-night vigil. Then, after warning the Moderator that what I wished to say was probably out of order as one should not defend a motion already defeated, I said, as near as I can recall: 'Moderator, I believe that yesterday's decision of the Assembly that we should retain the nuclear deterrent is the greatest tragedy in the history of this Church in my lifetime. For the Assembly said, and I am not speaking figuratively – this is the precise meaning of the deliverance they accepted – the Assembly declared that it is the will of God that under certain circumstances we should burn alive millions of our fellow human beings, and start a process over which we have no control, and which may result in the destruction of the human race. It may be that Commissioners were saying under their breath that they did not really mean this – they were just trying to frighten the Russians – but they would never be able to say that out loud because no-one has ever suggested that the deterrent would deter unless the enemy were quite certain that we were prepared to use it.'

I do not suppose my words had any affect on anybody and within a few minutes a tired Assembly had finished the day's business. I am reminded of the story of a Vietnam protester who sat on the pavement holding a poster. When he was asked what he was trying to do he replied: 'I am trying to stop the seventh war from now'.

Roger never saw any division between his work for peace and his life as a Christian within the Church, and he was constantly striving to integrate the two more closely. Perhaps the highlight of his achievement in this sphere was the International Peace Conference held in Portree Parish Church at Easter 1979. In the following extracts Roger outlines his programme for the conference to the Portree Parish Church AGM, and this is followed by two newspaper reports of the event: one from the *West Highland Free Press*, and the other, written by a participant Steve McBride, member of the Peace People of Northern Ireland, in the magazine *Peace by Peace*, which he edits.

Portree Parish Church AGM, 29 March 1979

This evening I have the very pleasant task of introducing you to a peace conference to be held in the Parish Centre this Easter, from the evening of Good Friday, 13 April to Sunday night, 15 April. I think the best way would be to pass round the programmes of the conference so that, after I have been speaking for a minute or two, you may ask any questions you wish.

As you will see from the front cover, we are most fortunate in having for our principal speaker Reverend Dr. Peter Matheson, a lecturer in Ecclesiastical history in Edinburgh, and the theme of the conference will be his new book, *Profile of Love – Towards a Theology of a Just Peace*. He was the principal speaker at a conference on Iona last year where there

36

was a wonderful gathering of men and women with an international reputation in the peace movement from America, Holland, Germany, Switzerland, and Northern Ireland, not to mention Scotland and England, but when I asked him whether he would lead a conference in Portree he said at once that there was nothing he would like better if he could find the time to do so.

I should mention in passing that he is the son of our own minister but that fact in no way influenced my decision to invite him, for I knew Peter long before I knew his father. One of the reasons I was so keen for him to come is that his ideas, and even more important, his quiet, courteous and convincing way of expressing them, are as different from my own as can be imagined.

We hope that most of you will join us for the whole conference, and, if you are able to do so, please let me know in advance if that is possible, so that we will have an idea of the numbers.

You will notice on the programme that there is to be a public meeting in the Parish Centre at 8 p.m. on Friday, that is, immediately after the Good Friday service in the Church at 7 p.m. If, for some reason, you are not able to join the conference later, we do hope that you will come to the public meeting and bring as many of your friends and relations with you as possible. There will be plenty of room. If we fill the hall we can have overflow meetings in the other rooms in the Centre.

There is one other way in which one or two of you may help us. We intend that all our conference guests should be accommodated in private homes. We have already had offers to accommodate ten of our guests in addition to offers of empty houses from friends who are to be away during Easter, but we still need accommodation for another two individuals. If any of you would like to accommodate them, then please let me know after the meeting.

It is difficult to know how to end this intimation as there is so much that could and should be said. There are no limits to the ways in which such a conference might develop and benefit us all, but if we receive and act on the guidance of the Holy Spirit then we can, together, move towards the ideas of peace within ourselves, and peace between the nations, ideals which are shared by almost every living creature in every country in the world.

I shall end, not with any words of mine, but with those Peter Matheson said at the conference at Iona last year. I came across this quotation in a copy of the newspaper of the Peace People in Northern Ireland, Peter said: 'We need not be, we are not called to be, ashamed of peace. Christ is not the beggar of peace. He is the Prince of Peace. The future is on the side of peace, and we are triumphant in that.'

From the *West Highland Free Press*, Friday, 20 April 1979, 'No Peace Without Justice'

The search for a new perspective on peacemaking in the contemporary world was the theme of a conference in Portree over the Easter weekend.

And Dr. Peter Matheson of Edinburgh University, principal speaker at the Conference, posed the question of WHO in the General Election campaign was discussing the fundamental issues of peace, war, and Britain's possession of nuclear weapons; WHO was facing the coming exhaustion of the conventional energy sources; and WHO was grasping the thorny problem of Northern Ireland?

Residents of Portree and Skye were joined by visitors from Glasgow, Edinburgh, Aberdeen, and other parts of Scotland, as well as from Northern Ireland, for the conference, which was based on Dr. Matheson's new book, *Profile of Love — Towards a Theology of Just Peace.*

Dr. Matheson said that peace had been too often understood in the weak, negative sense of the absence of war, of people just wanting to be left alone, unaffected by other people's problems. He charged that the Church had too often sought a shallow peace by encouraging people to accept an unjust status quo.

He declared: 'The Church is not the Church if it is not engaged in peacemaking. And you cannot talk of peace without talking about justice. '

In view of the problems of the modern world — ranging from the 'glaring injustices' of life in the Third World to the misery of life in many big city housing developments in Britain — there was an urgent need to find a realistic hope for the creation of a more humane society.

'We live in a world where the pressures in favour of violence are strong, seductive, and inescapable. What we need is a doctrine to account for the depth of these pressures and to show the possibilities of countering them.'

Another guest speaker at the conference was Steve McBride of the Northern Irish Peace People who described the work of the movement. He recalled the formation of the Peace People by Betty Williams and Mairead Corrigan after the deaths of three young children after a shootout between the British Army and the IRA. And he described how the movement is now working at grass-roots level to encourage people to overcome traditional fears and prejudices by working together to tackle their common problems. Mr. McBride said that the suffering of recent years had shown people in Northern Ireland the futility of their past divisions, and 'the obvious failure of violence to accomplish anything but increased suffering' had given many people impetus to seek co-operative, non-violent means of resolving their conflicts and tackling their common problems.

Participants at the conference also debated a wide range of issues, including that of the Church in peacemaking, particularly in regard to its attitude on nuclear disarmament, in respect of which some strongly divergent views were expressed. Other issues considered included the question of trade union power and its use recently in an apparently ruthless and selfish manner; the materialist nature of contemporary society, in which potential violence is always present in a view which values things rather than people and which tends to judge people by what they own rather than by their human qualities; and aspects of violence at the local community level.

Steve McBride's Easter Pilgrimage

To the west the land rolls off, its bleakness only slightly disturbed by small crofts, to the Atlantic swells of the island's west coast. To the east of Portree is the very sheltered loch, which remained mirror calm and clear throughout my stay, an amazing thing to someone used to the restless sea and continuous winds of Ireland's west coast and islands.

It was in these surroundings under the influence of the deep peace of the ocean and a land little spoiled by man, that a very mixed group from Skye, Glasgow, Edinburgh, Dumbarton, Aberdeen and other parts of Scotland, and from Belfast, met to discuss Peter Matheson's new book *Profile of Love: Towards a Theology of a Just Peace*.

The book came about as part of a search within the Church of Scotland for a new perspective for peacemaking in the modern world, a means of relating the element of love in the teachings of Christ to the personal lifestyle and to national and international politics.

These topics provided lively discussion amongst the diverse group at Portree, who had come to peacemaking through CND, Amnesty, the Church, Buddhist and other various routes, and who had been brought together for this weekend by Portree optician and long-time peace campaigner, Roger Gray.

In 1971 the Isle of Skye Peace Centre was started in a flat above the optician's shop in Portree. It had a well-stocked library of peace materials, plenty of pamphlets and posters, living quarters and ample meeting space. In relation to its size the Isle of Skye's Peace Centre's influence was extensive. A copy of the Annual Report gives some indication of its work. Activities included selling Christmas cards and calendars for UNICEF, Christian Aid, and World Wildlife Fund, to the tune of over four thousand cards with total receipts of more than £600 being sent to the three charities. Events included the peace conference already mentioned, and also on Hiroshima Day, Monday 6 August, four films were shown in Portree. A vigil was held in the church, followed by refreshments and singing to the guitar led by two Friends of the Peace Centre, one from Canada and the other from the USA. In the autumn a film show was held in aid of the refugees of Cambodia, and in January of 1980 Mary Gray reported on the work of the Peace Centre to a meeting of the Women's Guild of the Portree Parish Church.

Obviously the influence of the Peace Centre spread far beyond the bounds of Skye. It became routine for me to look around at every peace demonstration for the colourful blue and white banner of the Isle of Skye Peace Centre and the smiling faces of Roger, Mary, Ruth, and their friends. It always created an impression. 'My goodness, Skye, what a long way to come.' Or, 'A peace centre on Skye. I must visit it.' Countless visitors must have dropped into the Peace Centre over the years.

As he approached retirement age, Roger realized that he would have to sell the optician's practice, and with it the flat housing the Peace Centre. He hoped to realize his dream of integrating peace work within the local church, by suggesting that the Peace Centre be accommodated in the Parish Church. Here is his proposal to the Kirk Session, and a report of their reply.

Proposal to Portree Kirk Session that Skye Peace Centre should be accommodated in the Parish Centre

At the last Session meeting it was agreed that, rather than speak at some length on a new subject at the end of the meeting, I should write to each member to raise the question of the peace movement in Skye and the relation of the Church to it and to make two suggestions with which you will, I expect, all agree.

There has been an enormous increase in support for the peace movement in general, and the Campaign for Nuclear Disarmament in particular, both locally and nationally during the past year. In Skye this summer we have sold many times the number of badges and pamphlets than we have sold in the past twenty years, and many visitors from at least ten countries overseas have signed our petition and said how delighted and encouraged they were to find such an active centre in Skye. And ministers, elders and other prominent people who once lived here and were our principal opponents are telling us that they now fully support CND policies.

A few years ago our Kirk Session sent a letter to the committee on Church and Nation urging them to support unilateral nuclear disarmament and that letter had the unanimous support of the Session and so, unless and until we decide to change, that remains our policy. My present proposals are even more modest than that.

The AGM of the Skye branch of CND and the Peace Centre is to be held in the Parish Centre on Friday, 18 September. We are expecting many people from all over Skye and I hope that all of you will also be present, if only as observers. I would ask for the practical support of the Church in two ways. We are hoping this year to call on every house in Skye with a petition of the World Disarmament Campaign. This petition falls far short of CND policy but has the unanimous support of the General Assembly. So many Christians, and others, in Skye have been so distressed by the decision of the General Assembly to reject CND policy by a majority of over two to one, that it would be helpful if I could let our branch, know that this Session, as well as the whole Assembly, supports this petition, and that at least some elders will be taking it around the houses.

The other point is that I am hoping to sell my optical practice and in that case the Peace Centre premises may have to be moved and I would ask you to agree to the principle that, if necessary, the Peace Centre should have the use of one of the rooms of the Parish Centre. Probably all that would be necessary would be to have a large cupboard, with a lock, along one wall for our books and literature. That might be combined with the church library, to which many books have already been offered, that we have always planned to have in the Parish Centre. I need hardly say, that when needed, the room could be used for any other purposes, such as Sunday School.

I make these suggestions partly for the sake of the peace movement, but mainly for the sake of the Church for, as you may know, I believe that the new reformation which is necessary if any of the things or people in which we believe are to survive has already begun, and the quite incredible increase in support for the peace movement cannot be explained except in terms of such a reformation, and that these suggestions that I am making will help to enable this church to be used by the Spirit.

From the *West Highland Free Press*, Friday 11 December 1981: 'Kirk Final "No" to Peace Centre'

The Kirk Session of Portree Parish Church last Thursday re-affirmed its decision not to allow the Skye Peace Centre the use of a room in the Parish Centre. This means that the ten-year-old Peace Centre will almost certainly close down. Skye Peace Centre was started in 1971 by Portree optician Mr. Roger Gray who gave it a home in his Wentworth Street shop. Mr. Gray has recently retired, however, and as the shop space was no longer available, he applied to the Kirk Session – upon which he sits as an elder – for the use of part of a room in the Parish Centre. In late October, the Kirk Session met to discuss Mr. Gray's application and after heated debate they voted against offering a home to the Peace Centre by seven to five.

One of Mr. Gray's supporters on the Session, Mr. Brian Foreband, commented at the time, 'It seems a bit crazy for a church not to support peace.' But the minister, the Reverend John Ferguson, was adamant that he would dissociate himself from any decision favourable to the Peace Centre and the 'noes' carried the day.

At last Thursday's meeting of the Session, Mr. Gray attempted to get his decision reconsidered, but the Session made it clear that there would be no change of mind, and the matter was not debated or put to the vote again.

After the meeting, Mr. Gray said: 'As a primary aim of the Centre is to bring people together to work towards justice and peace, whatever their religion or politics, and as the Centre now seems to be causing discord rather than concord, it may be that the time has come for it to be discontinued.'

After Roger's death, Mary attempted to continue the dream of the Peace Centre, but it proved impossible, and with Mary's death in 1988 an era in the life of the peace movement in Skye ended. Roger's struggle within his local church was never easy and must often have been painful for both parties, but Roger had a deep, abiding faith that his labours were not in vain and that in the end peace would prevail.

In 1986 Roger's heart must have been gladdened indeed by the Church of Scotland's recommendation that a Peace Group be set up in every parish. Never one to waste time, Roger made many proposals of a most practical nature, and at the last Session Meeting attended by Roger, a committee was set up, under the convenorship of the headmaster, and duly reported that the proposals were accepted, and that a library of books on religious topics, including books on peace, would be established. Indeed, Roger's work had not been in vain.

CHAPTER 4

THE COURTS OF THE CHURCH

Although Roger would have continued speaking out as a Christian pacifist, even if he were a lone voice, he was also a strategist, well aware of the importance of political structures and decision-making processes. But for Roger, the Christian, the sphere of his involvement was the 'Courts of the Church' in Kirk Session, Presbytery, Church writings, and most significantly, the General Assembly of the Church of Scotland.

Perhaps the Quaker in Roger's nature responded to the challenge to 'Speak truth to power', for that, in spite of all its immense personal cost, is what he did, year after year. Each speech was carefully written out in advance, polished, prayed over, and then practised and practised until delivery was perfect. Even more remarkable were the times when he spoke 'off the cuff' without the time for preparation, simply responding to the call to speak and risking embarrassment.

He believed firmly in the power of the Christian Church united to change the world, just as fervently as he believed it was currently lagging far behind and even preventing moves towards world peace.

I have long been convinced that if the world Church, with its vast potential, and its peculiar access to the power of the Holy Spirit, had been in the vanguard of the peace movement, already the possibility of nuclear annihilation would be as almost remote as a return to cannibalism.

The following list shows the number of times Roger was sent as a Commissioner to the General Assembly, surely a mark of the respect his own congregation in Skye held him, and shows that he spoke on almost every occasion.

ASSEMBLY VISITS

1965   Commissioner: move motion against nuclear war.

1966   Commissioner: move motion on Vietnam

1967   Commissioner: move motion on Vietnam

1968   Visitor

1969   Visitor

1970   Commissioner: move motion on Vietnam

1971   Commissioner: refused permission to speak in debate on Vietnam

1972   Commissioner: speech on Church unity

1974	Commissioner
1975	Commissioner: move motion against nuclear war
1978	Commissioner: spoke on Iona Community Report
1979	Commissioner
1980	Commissioner: led 164 Commissioners in recording dissent against Assembly's decision not to debate nuclear weapons
1981	Commissioner
1982	Visited Assembly (Dr. Reid's motion on nuclear pacifism was carried by 255 to 153 votes)
1983	Visited Assembly (Lord MacLeod's unilateralist motion defeated)
1984	Commissioner: successfully moved motion on Nuclear Deterrence (Cruise Missiles had arrived at Greenham)
1985	Commissioner: voted on Report on Multilateral Conversations which was accepted; voted for motion by Dumbarton Presbytery calling for a study group on the Theology of Nuclear Weapons, which was accepted)
1986	Visited Assembly, saw Lord MacLeod's motion on nuclear pacifism accepted, supported by Maxwell Craig, Convenor Church and Nation Committee, and Norman Warnock.

The Church and Nation Committee of the Church of Scotland is the large committee responsible for bringing the concerns of international affairs and social policy before the Assembly every year. It is within the remit of the Committee to present deliverances on the subject of nuclear weapons and the Convenor of the Committee will bring forward a report on which the Assembly votes. It is in this context that Roger's first speech at the General Assembly is seen; proposing a counter-motion to replace a section of the deliverance.

General Assembly 1965 Report of the Church and Nation Committee

Moderator, I beg to propose the following counter-motion to Section Six of this deliverance.

Delete paragraph A and substitute: The General Assembly believe that nuclear and other weapons of mass destruction are wholly evil, and that there is no faith or principle, political or religious, which could be defended by their use, and urge Her Majesty's Government to renounce the manufacture, possession, use and even implied threat of all weapons of mass destruction.

Moderator, Fathers, and Brethren, I would not dare to stand

The General Assembly of the Church of Scotland in session — May 1984
Church of Scotland photograph by Anne H. Maxwell

before you this morning and, if I did so dare I should, I am almost sure, not be able to speak, were I speaking just for myself. I am able to move this motion only because I believe that I am representing, however inadequately, my millions of colleagues in the peace movement throughout the world and, in particular, the thousands with whom I have marched and lived, by day and night, on the road from Aldermaston, and my friends and colleagues in the Isle of Skye.

But that does not mean that this motion is intended as a form of protest or as a vehicle for a debate on pacifism. I am speaking, as responsibly as I am able, as a Commissioner to this Assembly, and I believe that this motion is the absolute minimum that could be devised on this subject by any branch of the Church.

I accept the fact — I hope that I accept everything that seems to me to be fact — that the reforms and reformations are not inaugurated by the hierarchy of the Church, and that Assemblies and Vaticans sometimes lie for decades, if not centuries, behind their saints and revolutionaries. In olden times we used to hand over our reformers to the state to be executed. Today, we condemn them to an even worse fate. We hand them over to the popular press and their reputations are

45

devoured by the wolves of Fleet Street.

But there comes a time, inevitably and invariably, when the Church moves at least part of the way along the road that is still being explored by its own vanguard, and I suggest that this motion contains the minimum advance that is essential on this issue at this time.

I must now try and make as clear as I am able what is not intended and then what is intended by this motion.

Firstly, then, this motion does not, in my view, conflict with any of the paragraphs of this section of the deliverance other than the one that it replaces. I am in complete agreement with the remaining paragraphs B, C, D, and E.

Secondly, this is not a pacifist motion. I am not asking the Assembly to say that it is wrong to kill a man. I am not even asking you to say that it is wrong to burn alive women and children by the hundred thousand, as we did one night at Dresden while their husbands and fathers were somewhere else fighting in their defence. Still less am I asking you to comment adversely on the war being waged by our allies in Vietnam.

Thirdly, this motion in no way conflicts with the Doctrine of Just War. I would remind you that that doctrine does not state that war is just. It states that all wars are unjust, unless it fulfils each and every one of seven conditions, and no nuclear war could possibly fulfil any of the last three of the seven conditions.

So much for what the motion is not.

All the motion does is to declare that nuclear annihilation is wholly evil, and to declare that the only way in which it can be declared is by renouncing all the means of waging it and, should others not follow our example refusing any nuclear weapons to be used on our behalf.

I think that it is safe to assume that we all agree that nuclear war is wholly evil and that there is no-one present who would be prepared actually to wage it, and that if this motion is opposed, it will be on the grounds that the weapons will be intended only as a deterrent and that the unilateral renunciation of them would increase the danger of their use by others. I do not expect anyone to argue that the things that, as a nation, we value most — freedom, justice and peace — could be defended by the actual waging of nuclear war.

I believe that when the history of this age comes to be written, if the human race is permitted to survive that long, it will be found that the deterrent theory was a grim and terrible illusion, but I have not time to argue the case in the ten minutes I am allowed to speak. If it is agreed that nuclear weapons should never be used but it is suggested that we should be prepared to use them in order to deter a potential enemy from doing likewise then, I submit, the whole onus of proof on the matter of deterrence is on the opponents of this motion. And it is clearly impossible to prove, even beyond all reasonable doubt, that the deterrent theory is true.

If, Fathers and Brethren, you will accept all I have said so far, I think you will agree that any possible case against this motion has already fallen.

I shall conclude by stating two of the positive reasons I have for proposing this motion. The first I shall present in the form of a personal reason, and the second concerns the life and witness of the Church.

I can imagine some terrible and terrifying things that could happen to my wife and myself. Our country could be occupied by a Communist tyranny; we could be tortured and killed in a concentration camp; or we could be reduced to cinders in a fireball hotter than the sun. These are terrible and terrifying thoughts. But the worst fate I can imagine for my wife and my-self is something that has already happened. I am choosing my words with the greatest possible care because I do not want to exaggerate. I suggest that every one of us, including of course myself, is a potential and professional mass murderer on a scale compared with which Hitler was a bungling amateur. The worst thing I can imagine — and it is happening at this moment — is to live in a country that has stated over and over again, in deeds if not in words, that we are prepared, with the help of our allies, and under certain circumstances, to burn alive hundreds of millions of our brothers and sisters in fireballs which are hotter than the sun and, perhaps, poison the rest of the human race.

The second and final reason I shall state concerns the Church. Every person in this Assembly has been ordained as Minister or Elder to preach and practise the Gospel. I am sure that we all love our Church so much that we would do everything we could to preserve its life and witness. At this time we are disturbed, to give just one example, and very rightly so, by the fact that, to an increasing extent, men and women are committing adultery and children are fornicating. But if men and women refrain from committing adultery and if children can be persuaded not to fornicate, and I pray God that such will be the case, it will not be because they have been lectured in morality by a Church whose hands are dripping with the blood of the babies we have murdered and mutilated, babies we are murdering and mutilating, and babies we shall murder and mutilate for generations to come, in order to test — simply in order to test — the devilish obscenities that man has invented since he discovered how to split the atom.

Fathers and Brethren, I am persuaded that at this moment, and through this motion, Almighty God is handing us a torch. It may be a very little torch, and in our uncertain hands, its flame may flicker and die. But I believe that it is a light at this

47

moment and that if we accept it the light will be seen, in a world that is in almost total darkness, from the skyscrapers of New York to the jungles of Vietnam.

I say that the world is in almost total darkness. But even I can see flashes of light in all directions. I believe that it is the darkness that precedes the dawn, the dawn of a reformation that our Father has already prepared.

Moderator, I beg to move the motion. It will be seconded by the Reverend Hamish MacIntyre.

By the mid-1960s people in Britain were becoming increasingly aware of the horrors of the war in Vietnam, and the extent of US involvement. Making plain the links between this particular war, and the underlying evil of all war, and the possibilities of nuclear annihilation, Roger spoke many times at the Assembly on this concern.

The General Assembly – Church and Nation Report – 30 May 1967

Moderator, I beg to move the motion in my name on page 142 of today's order paper: 'The General Assembly urge Her Majesty's Government to disassociate itself from American policy in Vietnam; to support U Thant's call for a permanent and unconditional end to the bombing of North Vietnam; and to work for negotiations based on the complete, if gradual, withdrawal of all American and foreign forces.'

Moderator, Fathers, and Brethren, I imagine that there have rarely been such preparations for a single debate in the Assembly as there have been for this debate on Vietnam, and I feel that now, we are not so much at the beginning of a debate as nearing the end of a dialogue about which a choice is soon to be made. I think, therefore, that my primary task is to state why I believe that if this motion is defeated it will be a disaster almost without parallel in the history of this Church, and that if it is accepted, we shall at least have started on the only road that can lead to international sanity, let alone international peace.

I suggest that the case for this motion can be proved on military grounds alone, for if a line must be drawn against the possible extension of Eastern Communism, that line should not be drawn across the centre of a country that threatens no-one, and that has been fighting for its independence against aggression, from Japan, France, and now America, for over twenty years.

To prove the case on political grounds is even simpler. American lawyers have stated that their country has no legal right to be waging war in Vietnam. The whole campaign is in flagrant violation of the Charter of the United Nations and the American Constitution, and is against all the international laws on which alone a community of nations can be built. I

48

think the last word on the political aspect of the case has been stated by Thich Nhat Hanh, the Vietnamese scholar. Thich Nhat Hanh is one of the spiritual and intellectual leaders of those Buddhists in South Vietnam whom we, the Christian West, are there ostensibly to defend. He is completely opposed to Communism and he says, on page 116 of his book *Vietnam: the Lotus in the Sea of Fire*: 'Many Westerners try to relieve themselves of the guilt for United States actions in Vietnam by maintaining that American troops are there only because of invasion from North Vietnam. That is not true and my friends from the West should not be permitted to take refuge in this myth. Serious infiltration did not begin until long after United States domination of South Vietnam was a fact, and the US-supported South Vietnamese government had refused to carry out the elections which had been agreed upon.' I sometimes wonder, even at this stage, if we all realize that the only Communists in Vietnam are Vietnamese Communists, and that the longer the war continues, the more are converted to Communism.

But it is not military or political considerations that are behind this motion. It is the moral aspect that has caused movements of protest to sweep the world like a fire, and that has caused from a quarter to a half a million Americans to march in New York on a single day, or, to come from the general to the particular, that has caused an American Quaker, husband and a father, to burn himself to death in front of the White House, because there was no other way in which he could identify himself with the agony his nation was causing in Vietnam, an agony which had consumed the mind of the Quaker before the fire consumed his body.

But it is the means by which the war is being waged that is really blasting the people of the world into action. There has been nothing in history to match the burning of village after village and their inhabitants, or the use of chemical warfare to destroy a million acres of forest. American scientists have begged their President to at least refrain from chemical warfare which may wreak permanent and irreparable damage on the country, and its long term effects on people is still unknown. We are bombing the principal towns of North Vietnam, and using anti-personnel bombs which are quite useless against the military objectives we claim to be attacking.

All this leads to the supreme question before this Assembly: 'What should we, the Church, do?'.

I suggest there are two things we must not do. Firstly, we must not ask the government of North Vietnam to negotiate while schools, hospitals, churches, villages, and even towns are being destroyed, and the inhabitants are being cut to pieces by the most revolting form of anti-personnel bombs that have yet been invented. We did not even discuss the German peace

49

proposals in 1940, but demanded the total surrender of all the German forces. All Ho Chi Minh asks is that American forces decide to leave Vietnam. He does not even ask them to leave immediately.

Secondly, we must not ask the National Liberation Front to negotiate while the entire country is being systematically destroyed, and their people are being burned alive and in a manner and on a scale that is too ghastly even to imagine, and by an enemy over 7,000 miles away, and an enemy supported by Saigon Governments from the notorious Diem regime to the present one under the Hitler-admiring Marshal Ky.

I hope it is unnecessary for me to emphasize that, like yourselves, I wish the NLF and North Vietnam would refrain from war and violence. As a Christian, I believe that they would attain their independence and peace more quickly and more surely by the sort of pacifism that Jesus preached and practised. But I consider it would be pure hypocrisy to ask them to lay down their arms, or even negotiate, until I have persuaded my fellow Christians in the West to end the war to at least the extent of restricting ourselves to military action only if and when attacked.

And so, Fathers and Brethren, I come to what I believe is the only course that the Church can follow if the world is to be saved from continuing to accept this appalling evil which may lead to the unimaginable horror of nuclear annihilation. I believe that we should tell our American friends that they are waging an unjust war and that an honourable withdrawal can and must be effected. The American President and his advisers are not devils, fiendishly plotting the mutilation and murder of the children of Vietnam, and it is estimated that a million children have been killed or wounded already. Our statesmen are ordinary people like ourselves, caught up at the focal point of hundreds of years of rejection of the simple humanity which lies at the very root of the Christian Gospel. And how can they extricate themselves, and the human race, if even the Church refuses to preach that Gospel?

We are often told that the Church is so weak that no-one listens to us any more. I suggest that if no-one listens it is because we have nothing to say, and if we do not speak on Vietnam, then, in my view, the world is right, and the Church has no real contribution to make to the nuclear age. I believe that, at this moment in history, the world is waiting for a lead, and that if we preach the Gospel everyone will listen. Some will love us and some will hate us; some will praise and some will persecute us; but all will listen. So will we speak? Will we apply the Christian Gospel to the situation in Vietnam, and say at least as much as is contained in this motion, today − now? I am sure that we should. I pray that we will.

General Assembly of the Church of Scotland − 31 May

1966 Report of Church and Nation Committee — Counter-motion to Section 2, Paragraph C of the Deliverance: (Delete Paragraph C and substitute the following):

'The General Assembly believe that the war now being waged by the United States of America and her allies in Vietnam is a danger to world peace, and that the methods being used are an outrage to humanity and must have an incalculable effect for evil for generations to come.'

'The General Assembly therefore urge Her Majesty's Government to cease to support United States activity in the war, and to work to obtain negotiations based on the complete, if gradual, withdrawal of all United States and other foreign forces.'

'The General Assembly believes that only in this way can Britain fulfil the role of Co-chairman of the Geneva Agreement, and work effectively for peace and stability in Vietnam.'

Fathers and Brethren, I have been amazed at the extent to which opposition to the war in Vietnam is growing, especially in America, and this tide threatens to engulf statesmen and politicians who wish to rely on the threat of nuclear violence within the concept of the cold war.

But the Church as a whole is not only lagging far behind but is in many cases opposing this world-wide movement towards pacifism. It has not yet been convinced that the astronomical sums now being spent on nuclear weapons could be used for the benefit, spiritual as well as material, of the developing countries.

But this motion is concerned with only one aspect of international affairs, the war in Vietnam.

One of the commonest and most effective ways of justifying evil and making darkness appear light is to argue that the situation is far more complex than it appears, and that those who take the simple view possess an innocence or idealism which is generally equated with stupidity. Thus, the opponents of slavery were told that we must have slaves so the economy of the British Empire would not collapse and, only last century, even the hierarchy of the Church defended the hanging of children for stealing bread on the grounds that law and order required such a penalty.

I suggest that fundamentally the situation in Vietnam is just as simple as the questions of slavery, and the hanging of children, and is as follows.

About a quarter of a million troops have travelled over 7,000 miles to wage war in a small country which desires only to become independent and to be left in peace. The methods of warfare used by the invaders are so barbaric that many people, including myself, do not really believe the stories of torture and atrocities, even when they appear in respected and

51

respectable American newspapers. But we have, alas, no option but to believe that our American friends and allies are using gas, to drive the Vietnamese out of their underground shelters, chemical warfare, to destroy trees, bushes, and even crops, so that they may be seen from the air, napalm, to burn them alive and, to crown everything, the unrestricted use of air power against the defenceless peasant population.

These crimes against humanity are sometimes excused by a comparison with those of the Vietcong. But at least the Vietcong are not bombing New York, or burning people alive in Washington. At least they are committing crimes only within their own country.

But, it is suggested, we should not be unduly concerned about the sufferings in Vietnam — after all it is just a small country and a long way away — but should consider global strategy. It seems clear that there are no limits to the extent to which the USA are willing to escalate the war, unless they can be dissuaded by world opinion, and one must assume that the Pentagon is thinking in terms of a Pax Americana, in which Communism is to be contained by armed intervention in countries moving towards Communism, and in which potential enemies in general, and China in particular, are to be ringed with nuclear bases and face the continual threat of nuclear annihilation. I consider such a policy as impractical as it is immoral but, if that is the view of the Pentagon, I have no doubt that they sincerely believe it to be in the best interests of the human race. But I recall that in 1940 Hitler believed, no doubt with equal sincerity, that he was offering Europe peace and stability for one thousand years. But that did not in any way lessen my objection to bombing Scotland and England, which I consider no more a crime than the gassing, and bombing, and burning and the use of chemical warfare against the peasants of Vietnam.

In order to discredit those who support the Vietcong for the same sort of reason that we would a David against a Goliath, our opponents often say that the enemies of negotiation are the enemies of peace. Whenever anyone makes that comment I long to ask him if he said that in 1940; did he in 1940, urge that we should negotiate with Germany? Did he say then that the enemies of negotiation are the enemies of peace? Of course there must be negotiations between the Vietcong and Saigon government, but I submit that, as Co-chairman of the Geneva Agreement, we have no right to ask the Vietcong to negotiate other than on the basis of the complete, if gradual, withdrawal of American and other foreign forces. We should use the whole of our resources to try and persuade our American friends and allies that they are waging an unjust war in Vietnam, and that an honourable withdrawal can and must be effected. There are thousands, if not millions, of men and women in America who are eager to help us in that task.

A few days ago I saw the film 'The War Game'. I had read so many accounts of it and am so conscious of the facts on which it is based, that I found the actual film almost an anti-climax — except for a single sentence. There was one sentence in the film that shook me to the core and I do not expect ever quite to recover from its impact. At one of the more horrific moments of the film we were shown a shot of charred unrecognizable bodies waiting to be destroyed in a furnace, as there were no facilities for burying the dead. And by their side was a pail about half full of wedding rings, the only means by which some of the bodies might later be identified. And the man beside the pail said, as near as I recall: 'This is what happened in Dresden'.

Fathers and Brethren. This, this, in perhaps a different form and to a different degree, is happening now. And, once again, it is the Christian West and, by the Christian West I mean you, Fathers and Brethren, and myself, who are, at this moment, burning people alive in Vietnam.

I believe that if we accept this kind of motion and its implications we shall open the door, and the only door, which can lead to the reformation of which we talk so often, a reformation which, I believe, our Father has already prepared.

I pray that the agony of our brothers and sisters in Vietnam will not be in vain.

Moderator, I beg to move the motion.

In 1975 the war in Vietnam ended, and the Church and Nation Committee had now moved on to discussing the theological arguments of the 'just war'. Roger, by now well known as an ardent campaigner, was back in the Assembly arena with a motion against nuclear war, surprisingly only his second such motion to the Assembly as is noted in the text, when one of Roger's friends commented 'not again', implying Roger's preoccupation with the subject.

General Assembly — May 1975

Moderator, I beg to move the motion in my name on page 167 of today's order paper: 'The General Assembly, believing that reliance on nuclear and other weapons of mass destruction is wholly evil, urge Her Majesty's Government to renounce the possession, use and even implied threat of nuclear weapons by us or on our behalf.'

Moderator, in view of a complaint of a Commissioner this morning concerning the frequency of motions on nuclear weapons, I think I should begin with a personal story. Yesterday a friend who had noticed the motion in my name on the order paper said 'not again', supposing this was one of my regular activities. In fact I have spoken on nuclear war at Assembly only once in my life and that was exactly ten years

53

ago. I am most flattered to learn that what I said then is so well remembered that I am supposed to have repeated it annually! Today I do not intend to repeat any idea that I used then.

If I were asked what was the most important lesson I had learned from my spiritual advisers in the last twenty years, I think I would reply that the most important lesson that I had learned was that we shall obtain no light or wisdom, and that we shall receive no guidance from the Holy Spirit, unless and until we act on the light we already possess, and this motion is an attempt to do just that, and, what I suggest, is still the most important issue facing us, despite the enormity of the problem connected with the third world, or with over population, or with pollution and the poisoning of the environment, namely the question as to whether or not we are going deliberately, and consciously, to kill millions of our fellow human beings, and then perhaps start a process which will lead to the destruction of the human race.

For the last few years the Committee on Church and Nation has discussed the Doctrine of the Just War and considered the issues which divide pacifists from non-pacifists, and I am convinced that we shall receive no further enlightenment from that debate unless and until we act on the area of agreement that already exists.

And so, Moderator, this is not a pacifist motion, but an attempt to state a belief and decide on action on which the whole Assembly, pacifist and non-pacifist, can unite. It was the late Lord King-hall, better known as Commander Sir Stephen King-hall, a submarine commander in the First World War, who was far from being either a socialist or a pacifist, and who argued from a purely military point of view who said of a decision by Britain to renounce the use of nuclear energy for military purposes: 'It would be a decision worthy of a people who whilst no longer a Great Power in a military sense are still a great nation. We are still the same people whose government led the crusade for the abolition of slavery; created an Empire and turned it into an ever changing Commonwealth, gave the world parliamentary democracy, led India to independence; offered union to France and – it is my prayer – may yet lead the world to nuclear disarmament.'

I do not think it is necessary to state all the arguments in favour of this motion, but I would remind the Assembly that the specifically Christian stand-point is not that nuclear weapons are dangerous and might destroy the human race, or that they are ineffective in that they cannot defend the British way of life, or whatever it is we are trying to defend. The specifically Christian argument is that by simply possessing or threatening to use such weapons we have already destroyed all the values that are worth defending. In the words of the

Christian group of the Campaign for Nuclear Disarmament: 'Reliance on nuclear weapons means spiritual death, not at some future date, but immediately — here and now!'

The main argument that is used against a motion such as this is the deterrent theory. One can argue for hours, and I speak from experience as to whether peace is being preserved in the countries which are still in peace because of, or in spite of, NATO or American nuclear weapons. But one finds at the end of the day that one has not come very far, as the difference of opinion depends not so much on one's interpretation of past or present history as on one's fundamental beliefs on the nature of God and the nature of the universe. But this motion is concerned only with British weapons, and I do not think that it can be seriously argued that peace is being preserved by British nuclear weapons, any more than we would argue that peace is being preserved by French nuclear weapons. And the contrary argument is that by our continuing possession of these weapons we are encouraging the proliferation of countries possessing the bomb, and I am sure that every member of this Assembly is as much opposed to that as I am.

One of the reasons why it is urgent that the leadership of the Church should declare their views on this great moral issue is that large organizations of the British public, including annual conferences of the British Labour Party and of the Scottish Labour Party — the latter unanimously — have already accepted motions that go as far as this one. I am not using this as an argument in favour of the motion — I would be the last person to argue that an idea is true because it is held by a large body of people — but I thought I should mention this to indicate the urgency of coming to a decision on this issue.

And so Moderator, I end by asking the Assembly what is, I believe, the most important question that can be asked of such an Assembly at this time. Brothers and Sisters in Christ: do you think that the time has come to declare that reliance on nuclear weapons is wholly evil and to ask Britain to set an example to the rest of mankind — to Israel, to Egypt, to India — or do you think that we should leave that declaration of faith to some future Assembly?

From 1975 onwards the subject of nuclear war was on the agenda of the General Assembly almost every year, and alongside this the tradition of a vigil on the eve or during the day of the Church and Nation debate became a regular feature.

Roger's report on the Assembly of 1978 was recorded in the previous chapter. The following year, 1979, saw significant moves in super power politics, with the Pentagon's decision to deploy cruise missiles in Europe, including at Greenham Common and Molesworth in England; and Pershing 2 in West Germany. This 'twin-track' decision was the signal for a significant upsurge in the peace movement, and it was generally expected that the 1980 General Assembly would hear a most significant debate on the international situation.

Everyone attending was stunned when a motion was passed forbidding any debate on the nuclear deterrent. Roger Gray then led the way in an almost unique occurrence in which he formerly tabled his Dissent from the motion. A total of 164 Commissioners lined up to have their dissent formerly recorded, a procedure which delayed the business of the day considerably, and showed the strength of feeling around the topic. The visitors' gallery was packed and a hum of anticipation grew as the Church and Nation report was presented. Roger's feelings on the matter are recorded in two letters to the Church of Scotland magazine *Life and Work*.

Life and Work   Correspondence Columns 1980

Sir

The polarization in the Church of Scotland is now complete.

At all times the Church and Nation Committee and the Assembly supported the war our allies were waging in Vietnam in spite of the murder and mutilation of an estimated million children and the use of chemical warfare against forests and land, and the part we were playing in the nuclear arms race.

The climax was reached at this year's Assembly when the element in the Church which, over the years, has increasingly tried to stifle debate on nuclear weapons or Vietnam — on two occasions they stamped their feet during the opening debate — succeeded in preventing any debate on the nuclear deterrent, although three quite separate policies were to be put to the Assembly and almost all those due to speak had not previously addressed the Assembly on that subject.

To the decision not to debate the nuclear deterrent a record number of 164 Commissioners asked their dissent to be recorded.

The Assembly then supported the view that the government be urged to maintain 'a British nuclear force'. And so our Church has decided, in Committee and Assembly, there are not enough nuclear weapons in existence and Britain should obtain bigger and better ones.

The evil of this decision is only equalled by its insanity. It is evil to risk the destruction of most, if not all, of the human race because we cannot stand the thought of being occupied by a foreign power, and it is insane to suppose that the British way of life, or Christian civilization, or whatever it is we are trying to defend, can be protected even by the implied threat of nuclear war. We have already lost our freedom, for it is not 'our Government or ourselves' who will decide if and when we are to be annihilated, but an American President who may be as bad and/or mad as Richard Nixon.

Our decision to follow Caiaphas rather than Christ will

make little difference except to ourselves, for the situation is so serious that if we had accepted unanimously the motion of Douglas Galbraith, or even that of Lord MacLeod, it is doubtful if it would have been sufficient materially to alter the foreign and defence policies of the Government. Only miracles, in the narrowest sense of the word can begin to meet the situation and it is the purpose of this letter to suggest how we might begin to prepare ourselves for such an outpouring of the Spirit.

I believe that the darkness of the leadership of our Church is another sign and necessary preparation for the glory of the reformation which has already begun. The outstanding feature of the Assembly week was the all-night vigil to which all Commissioners had been invited, held on the eve of the Assembly at three Churches, Catholic, Episcopal, and Netherbow.

The kingdom of heaven is here now. As, in my work as an optician, I sometimes have to say to a patient — all you have to do is to open your eyes, and you will see.

Life and Work Correspondence Columns 1980

Sir

The answer to our Question: 'Can a majority and the unilateralist minority in the Church now agree to differ for a while?' is No. A rapidly increasing number of Christians are now convinced that even the possession of nuclear weapons by any nation or group of nations is as insane as it is wicked.

Would you have advised the opponents of slavery or the hanging of children for stealing bread to agree to differ from the majority? The possession of slaves and the hanging of a few children cannot be compared even with the threat to blast and burn a few million children.

You then say, 'on both sides there is probably a legacy of the ill feeling about the way the issue was forced and settled.' Why? In my dealings with responsible churchmen including five ex-convenors of the Committee of Church and Nation, I have received nothing but courtesy and respect. In debate our opponents have been honest and honourable and I am aware of no barrier between us.

I realize that my oft repeated opinion that support for nuclear disarmament is essential to the Christian faith may cause pain, as the annual decisions of the Assembly cause me pain, but I see no reason why ill feeling should result.

At last two years later in 1982, Roger saw the beginnings of the realization of his dream, when the General Assembly by 255 to 153 passed a motion by a former Moderator, the Very Reverend George Reid:

The General Assembly affirm their abhorrence of war and their commitment to the Christian vocation of peacemaking, and call upon the Church of Scotland, as the Church of Christ, the Prince of Peace, to oppose the use of nuclear power for war-like purposes, to join with the rapidly growing millions, in other countries and in other faiths, who equally renounce the use of nuclear power for war-like purposes, and to press for the immediate cessation of the further manufacture of such armaments.

Recognizing the dangers inherent in the arms race and in recent developments in the attitudes and actions of the great powers, the General Assembly believe that particular efforts are called for at this time to reduce international tension and to start the process of disarmament.

Recognizing that many Church members believe not only the use or the threat to use nuclear weapons must be rejected for moral and religious purposes, whereas many others reluctantly accept that the nuclear deterrent is necessary to preserve peace, the General Assembly welcome the widespread discussion on peace and disarmament throughout the world, and urge Church members – (1) to pray constantly for peace; (2) to study the factors hindering the achievement of peace and justice; (3) to study the biblical teaching on repentance, reconciliation and sharing; (4) to work actively for peace and disarmament, through local groups, national campaigns and political parties.

The General Assembly learn with interest of the World Council of Churches Hearing on Nuclear Weapons and Disarmament and commend the report of this hearing, when published, to congregations and Church members for their study and attention.

Several of us had been holding a twelve-hour vigil of prayer and song outside the Assembly buildings. When someone rushed out with the news of the voting results, we were hugging each other and holding on to the railings in amazement. A minister walking past said, 'what's so surprising? You've been praying all day, and don't you believe in the power of prayer?'

For Roger the praying had been more like twelve years than twelve hours.

Roger's delight in 'ten miracles piled on top of one another' was reported in the *West Highland Free Press*.

West Highland Free Press, Friday 28 May 1982: 'General Assembly About-turn on Disarmament'

The General Assembly of the Church of Scotland last week adopted, for the first time in its history, a motion supporting unilateral disarmament in Britain – moved by a former moderator, the Very Reverend George Reid, and eventually adopted by the Assembly by the startling majority of 255 to 153. The size of the majority causes Mr. Gray as much joy as the fact that the motion was adopted.

'I am more than pleased – I just cannot believe it.' he says,

'It's like ten miracles piled on top of each other. And it just came out of the blue, out of a totally ordinary Assembly. In the morning of that day there had been such a childish debate on the Falklands. And then the subject of nuclear disarmament came up, and every person who spoke for the motion seemed to be giving the best speech of their lives.'

Mr. Gray reckons that the most crucial contribution to the debate came from last year's Moderator, the Very Reverend Dr. Andrew Doig, who seconded the motion.

'As far as I know he has never spoken in favour of nuclear disarmament in his life before', says Mr. Gray, 'but he stood there, upright as a ramrod, and made the most important speech. He said that in travelling around the country in the last year, particularly after having been confronted by young people, he had become convinced that the very credibility of the Church was in question if it did not reject nuclear arms. In renouncing nuclear arms, he told the Assembly, we would be joining the rapidly growing millions around the world who are doing the same.'

Mr. Gray is in no doubt about the importance of last weeks vote. 'It should have a colossal effect, certainly on the Church. If these things did not happen, that would be the end of everything. To quote Churchill, "It is not the beginning of the end, but it is the end of the beginning."

'Everything now has changed: the Church is now quite different. Donald MacDonald made a joke in his article about the Assembly in the *Free Press* last week, about a computer reporting that Jesus Christ was not present at the Assembly. It was a joke, but he was making a point.'

'However, that article was written in the middle of the Assembly. Had it been written at the end, I am sure that Donald would have agreed with me that Jesus Christ WAS present at the Assembly.'

Indeed the tide did appear to have been turned. In 1984 Roger made his wonderful 'testimony' on Greenham Common which appears elsewhere in this book.

In the General Assembly in 1985, motions came thick and fast as Roger was one of those voting on motions calling for multilateral conversations, and for the setting up of a study group on the Theology of Nuclear Weapons, both of which were accepted.

If anyone has campaigned longer in the General Assembly for nuclear disarmament, it is George MacLeod, founder of the Iona Community, and in 1986, Roger was present to see George MacLeod at the age of 90 have his motion on nuclear pacifism accepted. The motion was supported by Maxwell Craig, Convenor of Church and Nation Committee, and read as follows:

In this International Year of Peace, the General Assembly

calls upon Ministers and Kirk Sessions to set up groups within their congregations to study the implications for peace of the issues of justice, development, community and disarmament, including the nuclear freeze and other proposals.

As of now this General Assembly declare that no Church can accede to the use of nuclear weapons to defend any cause whatever. They call on HM Government to desist in their use and further development.

The dramatic moment then arrived, which was described in the *West Highland Free Press* by Roger, when Norman Warnock, who had previously opposed any disarmament motions, now spoke with all his heart in favour of this motion.

Roger died before any parish peace and justice groups had been set up, but he would surely have been encouraged by the growth in interest in the theme of Justice and Peace and the Integrity of Creation. The Lent study for 1989 entitled 'While Earth Endures' took up this theme in its pack, and over seven hundred copies were distributed to groups all over Scotland. The study culminated in a day conference in Glasgow City Chambers attended by over two hundred people, and jointly organized by the Catholic Justice and Peace Commission and the Protestant Peace Groups co-ordinators. Roger would have been glad that his twin concerns of ecumenism and care for the planet were coming together.

CHAPTER 5

A PEACEFUL RETIREMENT

Roger retired from his optician's practice in 1983, which simply meant that he had more time for campaigning. It was a time when disarmament campaigns were flourishing, although nuclear arms deployment was continuing apace. Cruise missiles had been deployed at Greenham Common and Molesworth; Faslane, and Coulport in Scotland were being extended in readiness for Trident missiles. The women's peace camp at Greenham Common had been established in 1981 and was still receiving wide media coverage; Peace Corner at Molesworth was the site of a permanent camp, the Peace Chapel had been built, the fence had been put up in all its obscenity: CND membership was at its highest and rising; the churches were making statements on disarmament of an increasingly direct nature. There was plenty to gladden Roger's retirement and keep him involved.

By now Roger's peace activities must have been known all over Skye. The World Disarmament Campaign had launched a petition for support of the UN Special Session on Disarmament, and although Roger privately thought it was rather weak compared with CND's unequivocal stance, he undertook to take it to every house on Skye. If you have ever visited a crofting community you will appreciate that was not simply a question of running down the village street popping leaflets through the doors. Croft houses are scattered and isolated, often with very rough tracks, sometimes accessible over faint cairned tracks over a peat bog. And Skye is a huge and rugged island many miles around with a large population. Nothing daunted Roger, and his trusty band had set out to visit every house.

Ruth Goodheir described to me how late one evening as dusk was drawing in, she and Roger were turning for home when they spotted a lonely cottage light some distance up the hillside. They debated whether to give just this one the miss, but thorough to the last they ploughed over the bog and the rocks to the house. The door was opened by a man who lived there on his own. When they explained their task, his face broke into a smile, he flung the door wide, showed them into a room where he had a great pile of copies of Lord Mountbatten's famous speech condemning nuclear weapons. He had been saving them for an opportunity when someone might help him to distribute them. Roger would not call that 'chance'.

By the time of Roger's retirement, Skye CND had grown, and a new branch was formed in Sleat in the south of the island. In the following speech which Roger made to them we have a fascinating perspective on his twenty-three years of campaigning.

I have been asked to say something about my faith and explain how I managed to remain cheerful and optimistic after twenty-three years of active involvement in the peace movement as, in so many ways, the international situation seems to get steadily worse and nuclear weapons multiply. Much of what I say will be in a Christian context, as that was the faith into which I was born, but I think that most of it applies to other faiths – the doctrine of re-birth, for example is as much believed and practised by Zen Buddhists as any evangelical Christians – or could be expressed within an agnostic, or even atheistic framework of thought.

Like the evangelist Billy Graham, I have had three conversions. The first took place fifty years ago. As far back as I can remember I attended church regularly but like most teenagers, I gradually lost interest in the church as it seemed irrelevant. Then one day I read an article by Leslie Weatherhead, a Methodist minister, and, over the next few years, read every publication of his I could find.

Eventually I heard him preach when he visited a church a few miles away. The church was full and his subject, in both the morning and evening services, was: 'the Humility of God'. His sermon seemed to be all about God, how this is God's world and will only work in God's way, and perhaps God's most remarkable characteristic is not absolute power or perfect love, but what St. Paul calls 'weakness' and 'foolishness', seen so clearly in both history and evolution, where it is not the heavily armed animals, but the rabbits that survive. Some scientists think that the only creatures that could survive nuclear annihilation are insects.

The next, Monday, Leslie Weatherhead addressed a packed hall, and his subject was: 'the Mind's Search for Security'. He spoke for over an hour on the hottest evening I could remember, on the theme that one of our chief driving forces was the drive for security, that the security offered by the world is an illusion, but that through belief in God there is security now and always. When it ended I was, in the narrowest sense of the word, 'born again', and feelings of powerlessness and insecurity were gradually replaced by enthusiasm and joy.

Twenty-five years later, after a breakdown in health, a world war, and some years working on the land, I visited Iona and had a second conversion. I realized that, at least for me, any solitary form of Christianity was impossible, and so became a member of the Iona Community. In some ways, this was the least immediate and dramatic of the conversions, but it included a far deeper commitment to such essentials of the faith as ecumenicity and prayer.

One of my earliest memories of George MacLeod, the

founder of the Iona Community, is of his enthusing about the Aldermaston Marches. At that time although a pacifist, I could see little point in them. Protesting against the possibility of nuclear war seemed rather negative, and not particularly praiseworthy.

And then occurred the third conversion, which was almost as instantaneous as Saul's on the road to Damascus. One day, if I remember correctly, I read in a newspaper that the Prime Minister, Harold MacMillan I think it was, said that American nuclear weapons in Britain could not be fired without our permission. The next day, the same newspaper reported that our Prime Minister had been in error and that the Americans could fire them as and when they chose.

As a result, I suddenly believed, rightly or wrongly, with a quite shattering intensity that, as a nation, we had lost our freedom — for what freedom is left if we cannot decide if and when we are to be annihilated? — without even our Prime Minister realizing it and, in a matter of hours. I seemed to rethink every social and political idea I had ever had. I cannot explain or even describe the process but not only did I not see the Aldermaston March as a useless and negative form of protest — such expressions as 'ban the bomb' annoy me as much now as they did then — but everything had turned upside down and become positive.

First I saw the bomb, which seemed already to have destroyed the freedom for which so many had fought and died, in all its evil and insanity. Then I became aware of the opposite, freedom, love, and life, and so gradually my faith in the positives developed. I hope this faith shows in the pamphlet I wrote about the 1963, Aldermaston March.

The events that followed the conversion were perhaps more remarkable than the events themselves. I was received most courteously by a meeting of our Kirk Session, although not an Elder at that time, and was later advised that the Church would not hold a meeting on the subject, but I was free to arrange a public meeting if I wished to. Although I had not studied the subject, and did not know of a single person in Skye who agreed with me, within hours I had booked a public hall and our minister had agreed to chair the meeting. I still find it almost impossible to believe that, without any previous experience, I spoke and answered difficult questions in public almost as fluently as I was able to do years later. The talk was later published as a pamphlet entitled: *Christianity and the Polaris*. I have not tried to sell copies for some years as I am rather embarrassed by its anti-Soviet sentiments. It was not until some years later that I visited Russia with people who understood the country, and realized that the primary motivation of the government and the people for their massive re-armament was not a desire to spread communism, but an obsession with two German invasions this century, and a determination to prevent a third.

Within days of the meeting the Isle of Skye branch of the Campaign for Nuclear Disarmament was formed. We had a long interview with our MP, Russell Johnston and, year after year, the Skye banner was seen and televised on the Aldermaston Marches. In the meantime I attended annual conferences in London. In those days, Canon Collins was the strong and colourful Chairperson, and Pat Arrowsmith a most powerful and dynamic activist. But most of all I admired the brilliant speeches and quiet mature statesmanship of Michael Foot. I still recall the magnetism of his expression 'cosmic arrogance' which he used to such effect in Trafalgar Square.

For a time we had local support, mainly from scholars, but the Cuban Crisis persuaded the population that the deterrent worked and support collapsed in Skye as in the rest of Britain. Ten years later, with national support at its lowest, we founded the Skye Peace Centre, which at one time or another had 245 members, or Friends as we called them, including twenty-three from eight countries overseas. This was a project of the CND branch and was wound-up eleven years later when our branch shared in the national revival.

On my retirement I twice visited Greenham Common. The first time Mary and I were entertained at the Orange Gate, and saw and felt the dynamic nature of life there. On my second visit I walked all the nine miles around the base, seeing every camp, and speaking to every member of the forces, American as well as British, that I met.

I expected to be overwhelmed by a sense of evil, but my experience was exactly the reverse. It seemed as though the nuclear weapons, protected from those they were designed to defend by fences and barbed wire (in some places five fences and entanglements deep) and those who believe in them, had no real power at all. It seemed that not only all wisdom and morality, but all power rested with the few women in the camps outside, and the multitude of men and women who, like ourselves, are behind them.

Roger was enormously thrilled by the setting-up of the Women's Peace Camp at Greenham Common. He visited twice — no mean feat from the distance of Skye. As we have heard on the first occasion in 1984 with Mary as his guide, he visited all seven gates and walked the nine hard miles around the perimeter fence, drinking tea with the women at the gates, listening to their stories, talking, laughing, chatting. The experience moved him profoundly, so much so that he made it the subject of a speech to the General Assembly in May 1984. One can imagine the attentiveness in the assembled gathering as Roger, the veteran campaigner, announced that he was not going to put forward the usual case for disarmament, but instead he would give his Christian testimony; and the surprise when the Greenham women were quoted as his inspiration. For Roger this was no cheap tactic, he spoke from the depths of his soul.

Speech to the General Assembly of the Church of Scotland, Church and Nation Day — 24 May 1984

Moderator: I beg to move the motion in my name calling on Her Majesty's Government now to pursue a policy of nuclear disarmament. It is nineteen years since I first spoke to an Assembly of my belief that opposition to the possession of nuclear weapons is an imperative of the Christian faith, since it is not possible, in practice or theory, to possess them without being prepared to use them. One of the lessons I have learned in twenty-three years active involvement in the peace movement is that few people are persuaded to change their views — and certainly not in five minutes — by arguments, and so, instead of arguing the case of unilateralism, I shall follow the example of Christians over the last 2,000 years, and give my testimony.

I am a born-again Christian, and like Billy Graham and many others, I have had two subsequent conversions. As a result, I recently retired from my work as an optician so that I might do more work in the peace movement. One of my first actions was to visit Greenham Common, as I just could not believe the stories I had heard of the determination and power, as well as the enthusiasm and love, of the few women who camped there.

I walked all the nine miles around the base, saw all the women's camps, and spoke to every member of the forces, American as well as British, that I met.

I expected to be overwhelmed by a sense of evil in the presence of weapons which could start a process which could lead to the destruction of life on this planet, and would certainly destroy all the values we were trying to defend, but could not feel any sense of evil, no matter how hard I tried. As I had my lunch in the woods in that lovely part of our countryside, sitting on the dry autumn leaves, with the sun shining, I realized that not only all wisdom and morality, but all power rested with the few women in the camps outside and the multitudes, of women and men, who are behind them. And I realized not for the first time, that whether we wish it, or even believe it, each one of us is, by our actions, choosing between the darkness of death and the light of life, because there is nothing in between.

In one sense that is not quite accurate because separating the one from the other are fences and barbed wire. Where I was sitting, in full view of the base, I was separated from the nuclear weapons by five fences and entanglements; and outer fence, with barbed wire above and below, then a path, then a barbed wire entanglement, then a third space, and a further barbed wire entanglement, then a much wider space and, in the distance, another fence with its quota of barbed wire.

We talk of sitting on the fence, but it is not possible to sit on barbed wire, and there is nothing between the devilry and insanity of possessing nuclear weapons, and the joy, and the freedom, and the love, and the glory, and the POWER of the Lord Jesus Christ, the King of all Creation.

Moderator; acceptance of this motion is not the end of the world, but I am quite, quite certain that it is the only possible beginning.

The campaign which began with the Aldermaston March came full circle in 1985, as in his 70th year, Roger joined the three day march from Stevenage to Molesworth.

Skye – Stevenage – Molesworth

This account of the first ever three day march to Molesworth, is a sequel to one I wrote in 1963 on the last Aldermaston March, published by the Isle of Skye branch of the Campaign for Nuclear Disarmament and entitled: *Skye – Aldermaston – London.*

On the road from Stevenage to Molesworth many marchers, hearing of the old man from Skye who had been on the Aldermaston Marches, approached me and asked me what exactly were the differences between the old ones and the present one. There are at least two major differences.

This time we were marching to a particular place – Molesworth – where, as a movement, we already are and, whatever the opposition and whatever the cost, have to remain until, for the first time, we cause the actual removal of new nuclear weapons which are already here, as at Greenham, or on their way.

Another difference is that twenty-five years ago we thought that the case for unilateral nuclear disarmament, whether argued on military, political, moral or religious grounds, was so unanswerable, and so self-evident, that all we had to do was state it, clearly and courteously, and it would be believed. How wrong we were! A quarter of a century later we are at last realizing the extent of the sacrifice and the depth of the commitment to which we are called, if the victory in which we believe is to be achieved. But however great the sacrifice or total the commitment, it is small compared with the joy of working together to ensure the continuing existence of life on the planet.

On the other hand, there is one striking similarity between the last Aldermaston March and the first Molesworth one. Then, we carried £2,000 worth of powdered milk for the starving children of Algeria. This time we carried, or collected, £25,000 worth for the starving in Ethiopia, to show that now, as then, we want the money being spent on nuclear weapons to be used to feed the hungry.

Good Friday — 5 April, 1985 Three three-day marches began from Leicester, Cambridge and Stevenage respectively, to Molesworth. I travelled to Stevenage by bus from Luton, where I had been staying with my sister and, before the march began, met and talked to Roger Spiller, national CND vice-chairperson, who once visited us in Skye; Gerry Hughes, a Jesuit Priest, who led a retreat for peace workers on Iona the previous month; and Pat Arrowsmith, a CND veteran who organized the first Aldermaston March.

Later Jenny Hunt, who worked in the Gorbals Group in Glasgow with members of the Iona Community, invited me to join a Christian group for regular services on the march. As a result, I became friendly with a small group which included John who had walked 700 miles across the USA on a peace march; Rob, who was training to become a Catholic Priest; and Tony, who had left the priesthood as he believed he could better serve the Church in that way. Tony was familiar with the music of Taizé and most expertly and beautifully led us in the musical side of our worship.

The weather was good and, while others continued to wear their outdoor clothes, I was in my shirt sleeves much of the day. We began the march through the main shopping streets, including a pedestrian precinct, and we were so happy and friendly that Stevenage looked even more attractive than would otherwise have been the case. Soon we had the first of many little services on the march. It was a Good Friday service of the Stations of the Cross. We took turns in reading, and sang the hymns and songs together. Part of this service took place during a meal break, on the sloping grassy bank on the side of the road, and I had the joy of reading to the assembled company one of the immortal sayings of George MacLeod, founder of the Iona Community, how Jesus was crucified, not in a cathedral between two candles, but outside the city wall, where the garbage was thrown, and that is where we should be, and that is what churchmen should be about. Another kind of service we would have was the reading of some Psalms, each of us reading a single verse, and ending with free prayer and all saying the Grace together.

Eventually, after a colourful and joyful march — there were many brightly coloured pennants and banners — and with music provided by a most lively band which was with us the whole of the three days, during which we made one new friend after another, and wended our way through the winding and undulating roads, we reached Biggleswade, and spent the night at Holmeade Middle School. Here we were treated quite superbly. As we were greeted with tea and hot cross buns, I remembered the vast tents of the Aldermaston Marches, with frost on the ground, and long queues for soup in the rain and dark outside. The Women's Capital Co-op were quite wonderful in the way they provided and served dinner at night and breakfast in the morning, in the school dining room.

Our Christian group gladly accepted an invitation to be driven to the local Catholic Church for a more traditional Stations of the Cross service, with a modern liturgy from the writing of Michel Quoist. To the surprise and delight of our hosts, as there had been much local opposition to the hiring of the school to CND, the priest welcomed those of us from the march, and said how he admired and respected our efforts for the peace for which all Christians are striving. We were driven back to the school for the meal which had been kept for us, after which, still sitting at the dining table, we had our evening service, including Bible readings and free prayer.

During that day we had walked about fourteen miles.

Saturday — 6 April

We all slept in a large well-aired hall, with plenty of windows and plenty of room. We found the floor hard, but probably slept more than we realized. We breakfasted from 7 a.m. and, after packing up our sleeping bags and any luggage we did not wish to carry during the day, had our morning service sitting in a circle on the floor. By then we were a compact group which any and everyone was welcome to join.

And so, quite overwhelmed by the wonderful way in which we had been treated and waited on by the Women's Work Co-op, and the affection with which they waved us farewell — I was reminded of the moving greetings and farewells of the congregation with whom I once worshipped in the Baptist Church in Moscow — we were bussed to Sandy, from where our second day's march began.

Again the weather was fine and I was in my shirt sleeves much of the day, contentedly walking through the pleasant countryside, fields, hedges, trees — in groups, but often singly — and crowned with a blue sky and gently moving clouds. There were about 2,000 on the march, and it was good to see the column stretching and curving along the country lanes, ahead of and behind us.

This was a prelude to the exciting moment when, in St. Neots, after crossing a rustic bridge and the wide open spaces of a large park, we were greeted and welcomed by the Cambridge marchers who had arrived there the night before. I was glad to meet again Margaret Johnson, veteran Greenham woman, and now a full-time worker for Ex-Services CND.

We then marched through the narrow and busy shopping street of St. Neots and, for the first and last time during the four days of the march and demonstration, I was angry and ashamed to be a member of the party. There was shouting from a few behind so loud that it seemed to be the whole of the march. Not only was it loud and ugly, with its constant 'out, out, out', but the slogans were either offensive or nonsensical. As I said to my immediate companions, it reminded me of the sheep in Orwell's *Animal Farm* shouting 'four legs good: two legs bad'. They must have realized our displeasure, as I did not hear them behave in that way again. In fairness to them it should be said that we were so elated by our welcome from the Cambridge marchers that it was difficult to contain our high spirits.

And so the march continued, a fine walk through the fine and gentle countryside. During the tea interval there was a curious little incident, typical of the way in which anyone like myself — in their 70th year, as they say in the highlands — was treated. I was sitting on the village green, alone as I wanted to be quiet, feeling more than a little tired, when a young man came up to me and, with some hesitation and embarrassment, asked if I was all right. When I said I was, he offered me an apple. I was about to refuse, as I did not particularly want an apple, which could well be the only one he had but, just in time, I saw the light and accepted and enjoyed it with the gratitude I felt.

Eventually we reached the park in Huntingdon where we were all to be accommodated in CND members' homes. I was one of the few to be housed at Alconbury, near the USAF base and, with three other marchers, was driven there by our hostess Christine, who had a young son, a very young and lovely daughter who was so disabled that she was unable to speak or stand, and two large dogs. It was a privilege to be a member, even for a night of such a household. The courage and dedication of Christine, who openly and actively opposes one of the most sensitive nuclear bases in Britain where, during alerts, the forces inside the base point their guns at those outside the base, right on her own doorstep, and with Americans from the base living in the same street, is yet another reason why, at least for me, I cannot imagine any kind of life outside the peace movement.

As I was to be the first to leave in the morning, I slept in a small room connected to the kitchen, on large square cushions. It seemed most luxurious and I much appreciated the few hours sleep.

During our second day we walked about fifteen miles.

Easter Sunday — 7 April

Christine drove me to the main gate of the USAF Alconbury base for the dawn Eucharist at 6 a.m. There were about a hundred there. The service was led by Kate McIlhagga who, with her husband Donald, are minister members of the Iona Community.

The early morning was fine but cold. Along the grass verge by the fence were the sleeping bags of those who had been on an all-night vigil. The cold from which the all-nighters had suffered was soon forgotten in the warmth and comradeship of the service. I would think that everyone present, from Quaker to Roman Catholic, partook of the Communion bread and wine. I was particularly moved by the singing of the Lord's Prayer, a quite elaborate rendering which once again, was so well led by Tony. The service ended in the same way as our little services on the march, by everyone holding hands and saying the Benediction together. Kate invited me to a second breakfast and drove me to her manse in St. Ives, a few miles the other side of Huntingdon, from where the last day's march began.

By now the weather had broken and it was cold and wet for most of the day. We marched to the Alconbury base, which I was passing for the third time in twenty-four hours. Outside the main gate we stopped and, holding hands, made our column stretch as far as possible. By now there were about 500 of us and we continued to Molesworth.

The lunch break was on an exposed path between two fields and the wind, from which we had no shelter, was added to the cold and rain. This made even more welcome the eggs and sandwiches and, best of all, the soup and tea, all supplied by a Dutch catering firm who fed us throughout the march and gave all their services free. And yet, so paradoxical is life, it was after that meal, the coldest, wettest, and windiest part of the three days, that we were the most lively and cheerful. The band which had accompanied us ever since Stevenage, seemed to take off and led us not only in singing, but also in dancing.

On the road again I met and walked and talked with Bruce Kent, who pushed a pram which contained wheat for the starving in Ethiopia all the way from St. Neots to Molesworth. After being interviewed and photographed by various reporters, he told me, among other things, that Gerry Hughes, the Jesuit Priest, was going to obtain more experience of the movement by working, for a short while, on the staff of national CND.

The lovely lanes and villages were rather marred by ugly notices telling CND to go home, but there was only one unpleasant incident. Outside a village pub there was a small group of disreputable people shouting insults. They, in fact, looked just like the false image the popular press paints of us! A few police separated us, but I do not know whether they were to protect us from them or them from us! Certainly no-one seemed to want to make a move in either direction. Apart from that we received only courtesy from everyone in the area I saw. It often seemed, from the expression on their faces, that they were amazed to find that nearly all of us were normal respectable people like themselves.

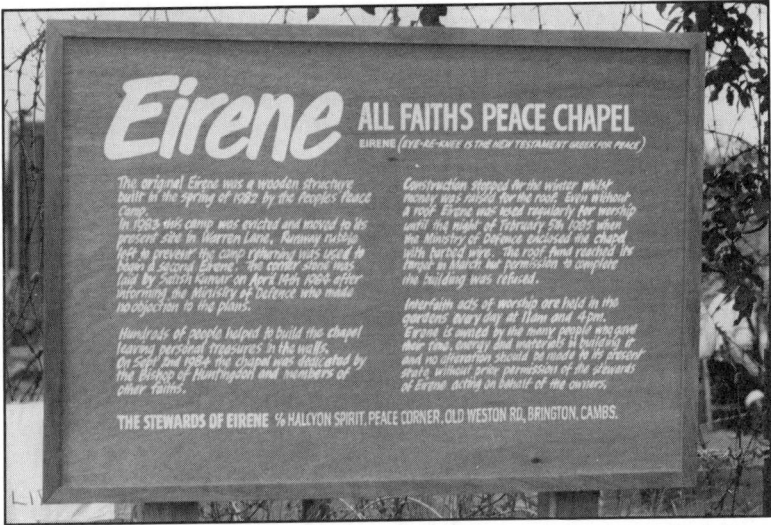

Eirene **ALL FAITHS PEACE CHAPEL**
EIRENE (EYE-RE-KNEE IS THE NEW TESTAMENT GREEK FOR PEACE)

The original Eirene was a wooden structure built in the spring of 1982 by the People's Peace Camp. In 1983 this camp was evicted and moved to its present site in Warren Lane, Runway rubble left to prevent the camp returning was used to begin a second 'Eirene'. The corner stone was laid by Satish Kumar on April 14th 1984 after informing the Ministry of Defence who made no objection to the plans.

Hundreds of people helped to build the chapel leaving personal treasures in the walls. On Sept 2nd 1984 the chapel was dedicated by the Bishop of Huntingdon and members of other faiths.

Construction stopped for the winter whilst money was raised for the roof. Even without a roof Eirene was used regularly for worship until the night of February 5th 1985 when the Ministry of Defence enclosed the chapel with barbed wire. The roof fund reached its target in March but permission to complete the building was refused.

Interfaith acts of worship are held in the gardens every day at 11am and 4pm. Eirene is owned by the many people who gave their time, energy and materials to building it and no alteration should be made to its present state without prior permission of the stewards of Eirene acting on behalf of the owners.

THE STEWARDS OF EIRENE % HALCYON SPIRIT, PEACE CORNER, OLD WESTON RD, BRINGTON, CAMBS.

Peace Corner, Molesworth 1985

Michael Szabo

And then the great moment towards which we had been marching for three days arrived. We reached Peace Corner Molesworth. The gardens our colleagues had made were surrounded and the chapel, not yet roofed, they had built was separated from us by barbed wire about six foot deep, with about thirty police within and around it. All this did not deter our colleagues who, twice daily, held an All Faiths' Service outside the barbed wire. Nor did it deter the daffodils which grew under or the birds which flew over the wire.

And what a reception we had. I was most warmly welcomed by Jenny who, with her two young children, had marched the first two days, and had done invaluable work keeping the Christian group together and organizing our many services, and Reg Comley, treasurer of national Christian CND, and member of the Iona Community. They offered to carry me over the mud, along the Eastern Bridleway, to the field with all our marquees! But all my tiredness had vanished, and I felt I could go on forever. The Bridleway, by the side of the fence, was very muddy. There were people everywhere and, right up against the fence, police every few yards.

The marquees where we were all to sleep all had thick matting, and I soon found the one with the floor covered with the luggage from our march. Being an old campaigner I made a space for sleeping well away from the opening and against the side of the tent. Almost immediately, by one of the many little miracles with which such marches abound, I saw John and

Rob, and cleared a space for them on either side. We then explored the site and found the tent where a thousand meals were to be served, in two lots of five hundred, by our Dutch catering friends. There chaos reigned. We three worked as a team and not only obtained food quite soon, but even found a few inches of ground on which to sit and eat it. The vegetarian meal consisted of three separate foods in three compartments on the same plate. Whenever we entered a tent we had to remove our boots or shoes, as they were caked in mud, and we had to sleep in the tents. The first time I left mine at the entrance, and, when I returned, there were dozens of others. So thick was the mud, one could not tell even whether they were black or brown, and it was many hours before I realized that the shoes in which I left Portree were not the ones in which I was returning!

Soon it was dark outside, but the outside of the marquees were well lit by electricity. Now coaches were arriving in their hundreds and people in their thousands, prepared for an all-night vigil. Meanwhile our tent was quite full of bodies. There was no path anywhere and, if we wanted to leave, we tried to stand on people's feet rather than their heads!

Before sleeping I went outside, in the rain and cold, and, by another of those little miracles, the first person I met out of the thousands was Margaret MacPherson, the first secretary of Skye CND, looking wet and cold, who had come by CND coach from Glasgow with three others from Skye, and intended to stay on the vigil outside. Later in the night, and again in the morning, she walked through the mud to Peace Corner.

During that day we walked about eleven miles, a total of about forty miles in three days.

Easter Monday – 8 April

During the night it poured with rain. Several times I thought I saw lightning, but learned later that it had been a very powerful searchlight from a helicopter hovering over the base. Sleep was not easy because of the noise of wind and rain, the occasional drop of water on one's face, and, not least, wondering how our colleagues outside were coping with the elements. Dawn broke and we arose and breakfasted in another marquee. Again we were grateful to our Dutch catering friends, and their excellent porridge, with two sandwiches, tea and fruit, and a sandwich I had kept from a previous meal, lasted me all day. The weather was cold, and raining on and off all day. The night's rain had turned the paths around the base into a sea of mud, in many places over the top of my shoes.

I walked all around the base, anticlockwise, a distance of about seven miles, as in the north and south the route lay along roads some distance away. In places there were paths across fields, well marked and roped off. National CND showed great wisdom in supplying many neat and clear notices saying

72

that CND asks everyone to keep off the growing plants and on the path. All along the route policemen and women were stationed, often in pairs.

Although wet and muddy, it was a pleasant walk, tiring, but never monotonous varying from road to path to mud, and with the lovely little village of Molesworth. As always I have only praise for the behaviour of the police. As I passed them I normally bid them 'Good morning' and, almost always, they smiled and replied, 'Good morning, sir. Are you all right?'. By the time I was half way around the base I was really tired, and finding it increasingly difficult to cope with the mud, sometimes holding on to the rope at the side of the path, or the barbed wire on the other side. All the police with whom we had conversations made it clear that they both admired and respected the efforts we were making.

At last I reached Peace Corner where thousands were collected and saw, once again, the gardens, the barbed wire, the chapel, and police everywhere.

Peace Corner, Molesworth

David Maxwell

It is clear, from the aerial photo published in *The Times* the following day, that the ground on which the chapel is built has no military use whatsoever and yet, within and around it were about thirty police and, between us and them, a barbed wire entanglement. Standing right up against the wire were two nuns, motionless and silent.

The chapel had been dedicated by the local Bishop, and

Bruce Kent was to lead a service there at 2 p.m., but I had to leave to catch the bus to Glasgow. It had taken me three hours to walk — and paddle! — the seven miles. So, once again, I walked to the tents on the Eastern Bridleway, bordering the high perimeter fence, the whole day guarded by 2,000 police, and enclosing fields which until a few weeks ago, were growing wheat for the starving, but were now being prepared to house the greatest obscenity the human mind has ever devised.

Back at the marquees, I watched Margaret MacPherson being televised, walking through the muddiest part of the field they could find. She was photographed walking with her interviewer three times, from the front, from behind, and then from the front again, but with the camera pointing at her feet, and a recorder near the ground to pick up the sound of the mud. The film was shown on BBC Breakfast Time the following day, with a film of Fenner Brockway, also at Molesworth, and now 96 years old.

And so the three or four mile journey back to the coach began, first in mud and then country lanes. I was burdened by my double sleeping bag which was quite heavy as it contained all my spare clothes and papers. When I was sliding about in the last stretch of mud trying with increasing difficulty not to fall over, a stranger passed and, with hardly a word, took my luggage and carried it on his shoulders, above his own large and bulky, and probably heavy rucksack, until we reached dry land. In the meantime Margey who, with Margaret MacPherson, Dougie and Jim, had travelled from Skye by bus the previous day, overtook me and, looking puzzled, asked if the stranger was a friend of mine. I replied: 'I have never met him before, but he is a friend now'. By then I was really tired and my friends from Skye helped me to carry my luggage, or even carried it themselves in addition to their own, all the miles to the bus.

The weather improved and the walk was fascinating as in every direction we could see paths and roads covered by thousands of demonstrators. We were told the total number of buses was 560, and the total number of demonstrators about 20,000. The whole countryside seemed alive with these colourful marchers, some still carrying their bright pennants. As we passed hundreds, going in the opposite direction, I was again struck by the fact that all of them looked so average and normal, quite indistinguishable from most other people.

The story is told in Huntingdon of two small boys, whose parents were housing several marchers, eagerly awaiting the arrival of the punks and dropouts of whom they heard so much. But, alas, the visitors were quite ordinary people, like their parents, and the disappointed boys are still looking for the punks!

During that day I walked, and paddled in the mud, about ten

miles., seven miles around the base and three miles to the bus, a total of about fifty miles in the four days.

Tuesday — 9 April 1985

We reached Glasgow after midnight and Philip who was in charge of the party, and whom I had not met before, slept four of us in his large-roomed flat and, for the first time since I had left Luton four days ago, I slept in a bed, but only for four hours, from 2.30 a.m. to 6.30 a.m., when I had breakfast and left to catch the bus to Portree. I travelled back with Margey, who had spent all Sunday night out in the wind and the rain, commuting between the marquees and Peace Corner, where there were torches and a fire burning, as part of a massive all-night vigil, and we spent our time on the bus either reliving our adventures or sleeping.

And so, as I wrote in the last sentence of my pamphlet on the 1963 Aldermaston March, 'we returned to our home towns to carry on the fight, quietly, but continuously, until our country renounces this appalling devilry and, once again, as has so often happened in the past, leads the world forward to the next stage in political evolution, a stage in which nuclear annihilation would be as unthinkable as cannibalism'.

What an insight into Roger's sheer courage and determination, in his 70th year to endure fifty miles of fun, happiness, hardship, and endurance. Roger's paragraph in that description, 'However great the sacrifice or total the commitment, it is small compared with the joy of working together to ensure the continuing existence of life on this planet', perhaps sums it up. With every cause Roger undertook that joy and enthusiasm shone through and made it a pleasure to be associated with him.

CHAPTER 6

A FIGHTING FINISH

On 19 May 1986 Roger Gray was arrested and charged with breach of the peace. It was almost in spite of himself, and against all his most reasoned arguing. For some three years since I had become involved myself in non-violent direct action, Roger and I had a continuing argument about civil disobedience. It wasn't that Roger didn't agree that there were occasions when Christians were called to obey the higher law of God rather than the law of the land. Rather it was that he felt that the time was not right, that the democratic processes still worked, and that it was not an effective form of protest. And yet all the time he was questioning, seeking, and fascinated by the arguments which many peace protesters were raising.

Roger had a tremendous respect for those who had made a decision in conscience to break the law. I remember his enthusiasm for the film *In the King of Prussia*, which we watched together during one of the all-night vigils in Edinburgh. This film was about the 'Plowshares 8', a group of Christians, including Daniel Berrigan, many religious and priests, who broke into the GEC factory in the King of Prussia in the USA and were arrested hammering the nose cones of missiles. When charged, their defence was that they were beating swords into ploughshares! Roger delighted in the defence in conscience they put forward, but always argued that that was not right for Britain.

His fascination remained however, and when I was arrested on a peace protest and finally went to prison for five days he couldn't have been more supportive. In June 1985 Roger attended a week entitled 'Civil Disobedience, Christian Obedience' at Iona Abbey, and moved among the participants in his inimitable way asking penetrating questions with a deceptively childlike innocence.

Thus full of questions, seeking, debating within himself Roger came to the Pentecost service on 19 May.

Christian CND had planned a peace witness at RNAD Coulport where Polaris nuclear missiles are stored, and where vast extensions are being made to accommodate Trident. Our worship was celebrating the coming of the Spirit at Pentecost and we had sent copies of our liturgy to the Chief Inspector of Police and to the Base Commander, so we were well and truly expected, as the double row of MOD police standing shoulder to shoulder across the gate amply demonstrated.

Our liturgy moved from penitence for our complicity in the arms race to triumph and joy in the power of the Spirit. During

76

the singing of the final hymn 'Be Not Afraid' our intention was to walk triumphantly singing through the main gate of the base, bringing the life of the Spirit in place of the power of darkness. However, it was obvious that the strong police presence made this impossible, so we followed our alternative plans. Eighteen of us chained ourselves together with padlocks on to long chains, threw the keys away into the loch, walked forward to face the line of police and then knelt in prayer across the gateway until we were arrested.

Roger, firmly determined not to be arrested, was standing watching with Mary and Ruth Goodheir by his side. At the point where we threw the keys away, and began to walk forward, he suddenly bundled up his coat and, thrusting it into Mary's arms, saying 'I can't stand this any more', he walked forward and joined himself on to the end of the chain, kneeling in prayer at the feet of the police along with the rest.

His action was totally spontaneous and unpremeditated, so much so that Mary's comment was 'Well, I wish he had told me he intended to get arrested! He has all the money — and he's got my glasses! How are we going to get home?'

Roger didn't regret his action for a moment. In the words of Ruth Goodheir 'When he got arrested, he was grinning all over his face. He looked just like the cat who got the cream.' The women were all taken to Helensborough police station to be charged, but the men were taken to Dumbarton, and so I didn't hear from him again until later that evening when we had all been charged and released. The telephone rang, there was the usual long stuttering pause, and then Roger's voice saying 'I've just been in heaven. I should have been in the cells long before this. Breach of the peace; it's wonderful; imagine that — breach of the peace. Just wait till we get the chance to speak in court. Why are the prisons not full of Christians breaching the peace?'

He was really looking forward to his trial and wrote or phoned me several times asking whether he should have a lawyer, what the court procedure was like, when he could speak, what prison was like — 'I couldn't possibly pay a fine for breach of peace; I'm keeping the peace.' Sadly, Roger died on Iona before he ever got to court.

My own trial was on the same day that Roger was to appear, and so I thought carefully about the defence I would make, as I felt so strongly that I would be speaking for Roger too. My own intention had been to present a good strong legal defence based on the Geneva Convention, the Genocide Act, and some other points of legal detail. The more I thought about it, however, the more convinced I became that Roger would have wanted to defend himself solely on grounds of his Christian conscience. And so with an amazing feeling of Roger's presence with me, I prepared our defence and presented it before the sheriff in Dumbarton Sheriff Court.

Coulport – Pentecost 1986

© Craig M. Jeffrey Ltd., Helensburgh

I stand here today very conscious that another should have been at my side. I speak of Roger Gray, lifelong peace campaigner and fellow member of the Iona Community who died very suddenly on 21 October. He would have been on trial today in this court and I can do no better than to quote Roger's words, as written in the *Coracle*: 'For the first seventy years of my life I have kept the laws of the land, believing it was right to do so, but on that day of Pentecost, I believed, with the others, I was called to make that particular witness to oppose the cosmic powers of evil which, if not overcome, will lead to the destruction of life on this planet.'

Roger said it was a privilege to be arrested, and was looking forward eagerly to making a Christian witness today. He stands here beside me.

Like Roger I am a deeply law-abiding person, although this may come as something of a surprise in this court. These are the laws which constrain me:

Firstly, as a member of the Iona Community, I promised to adhere to a five-point rule which includes a commitment to peace. The rule says: 'We believe that the threat caused by the existence of nuclear and other weapons of mass destruction is morally indefensible and that opposition to their possession is an imperative of the Christian faith.'

Secondly, the law of the General Assembly of the Church of Scotland plainly states: 'The manufacture, development and use of nuclear weapons is morally and theologically wrong.'

Thirdly, as a Quaker, I am bound to 'live in the virtue of that light and power that takes away the occasion of all war.'

In response to that Christian imperative and in the strength of that power, I prayed at the gates of Coulport. I prayed for forgiveness for my implication in the war machine; I prayed for deliverance from evil design and destructive hatred; I prayed for our beautiful, fragile, threatened planet. And I prayed that I might have strength to work for real peace.

This court is subject to the law of God, as shown by the value placed on the oath. The law of God is clear, and so I plead my innocence before that law.

I was sentenced to a £30 fine, which, with Roger as my mentor, I refused to pay and went to prison for seven days, of which I served five.

Roger died of a heart attack at the age of 70 on Iona, during Community Week, 1986. Apart from the fact that Mary wasn't with him, few deaths could have been more fitting, or indeed more joyful. The Community was in the process of rewriting its Peace Commitment to bring it more up-to-date, to include issues of social justice, to say more about the environment, and above all to sharpen it up and make it a clearer, more unequivocal statement of belief. As the Peace

Commitment is part of the Rule of the Community and had been adopted unanimously in 1966, we were striving yet again for unanimity with all the careful listening, discussion and understanding that involves. Roger had been in it up to his neck with a steady flow of letters, phone calls and passionate lobbying, particularly over the wording of the statement on nuclear disarmament. On this particular October morning members were crammed into the Coffee Shop across the road from the Abbey, seriously considering the final draft statement. Roger had just made an eloquent and impassioned speech on the subject of the political ineffectiveness of nuclear weapons, when he sat down suddenly, said rather apologetically that he was feeling faint and collapsed and died. Surrounded by some of the people closest to his heart, in a place he loved dearly, reflecting on a subject most important in the world to him, what better way of dying could there be?

He was laid out in the small Michael Chapel behind the Abbey and that evening we held a short service of thanksgiving for his life.

My first thoughts as I eased my way into the throng of friends and saw Roger's body laid out was how very tall he was — a man of great stature in so many ways. Roger's death and presence there in the midst of us all made the communion of saints a reality.

Of that simple service of praise the verse that will always remain with me was:

> **Those who die on the march shall renew their strength,**
> **they shall mount up on wings as eagles,**
> **they shall run and not be weary,**
> **they shall walk and not faint,**
> **help us Lord,**
> **help us Lord in your way.**

The funeral service on Skye was conducted by Roger's great friend the Reverend James Matheson. The tribute which he paid to Roger moved many in its accurate capturing of the essence of his life. It was written out lovingly in a fine scroll which was given to Mary, and I quote it here in full.

A Tribute to Roger Gray

Roger Gray was a unique gift to us. He made a special mark on our community on Skye and in this church where he was an elder. It is with great thankfulness that we remember him today.

The last time I was with him, a few weeks ago, we were taking part in a meeting about World Peace. That, as we all know, was his consuming interest. There was no distance he would not travel, and no sacrifice he shrank from, to promote peace. There are earnest devotees of good causes whose determination comes out in a grim, defensive attitude to the

80

unbelieving world around them. Not so Roger. He was always happy, always positive in his enthusiasm. In lean times and in good times for the Peace Movement he radiated the same hopefulness. To him, the building of peace was a direct consequence of his faith in Christ, and he knew in the end it would not fail.

We all admired the remarkable tenacity he showed in overcoming his speech handicap. It never prevented him from taking his full part in any company. It takes some courage to intervene in debate in the General Assembly of the Church of Scotland. Roger did, again and again and was listened to, especially in recent years, with increasing respect. Many a time I felt proud of his fresh and penetrating contributions. It was the spirit of the man, sincere and childlike – in the best sense – and so clear in insight, that shone through.

In controversy, and Roger was often controversial, he was always gracious. He had generous thoughts, even praise for those who opposed him. I recall him saying to me one time, in a kind of wonder at the mysterious ways of God, 'It's strange: some of the very nicest people in this place are army and navy men!'

Roger died on Iona. Where else would he have chosen to die, the Iona Community was a main source of his strength and joy. When the fatal attack came, he was actually taking part in a discussion on peacemaking. What else would he have wanted to be doing to the end? At the age of 70 having lived his life to the full, leaving a Christian witness we have been privileged to see and hear, he has gone from us. It was said about one Bible figure, in the simple language of the Authorized Version, 'he was a good man, full of the Holy Ghost and of faith.' Roger was not a conventional Christian, but in anyone's book he was a genuine disciple of Jesus, a good man: full of the spirit, full of faith. In the same faith we give thanks for him, and commit him to the God and Father he loved and served. We believe, that the offering of his life, which he gave with such total dedication will be accepted, and will be part of God's final Kingdom of Peace.

There is no way we can measure the value of Roger's life to so many who knew him, nor of estimating the number of hearts transformed, minds challenged, falterers inspired by his actions. Ebullient, hilarious, contemplative, outrageous, unswerving, passionate, humorous, joy-filled, childlike, prophetic, strong man of God – Roger Gray. If these writings can give some small reflection of the Roger we knew, then this small work is not in vain. But reading this is not enough: I can almost see Roger shaking his head as we read and winding himself up to say 'Yes, but what are you going to do now?' Remember the good man or woman is of action, prayer, and politics.

One of Roger's great friends in the Iona Community,

George Charlton, wrote this tribute to Roger, in the Iona Community magazine, the *Coracle*, and I quote in part.

Roger Gray, Soldier of Peace

Roger lived and died fighting for peace. He was a Soldier of Peace, a *Miles Christi* in St. Paul's vivid phrase.

Now a Soldier of the Queen will throw his body against the enemy and, if necessary, will kill to achieve his objective. A Soldier of Peace however, throws his body against the forces of destruction and, if necessary dies to save life — even the life of his enemy.

Roger certainly threw his body into the Campaign for Nuclear Disarmament. It is humbling and exciting to realize that he was in every major peace protest from the Aldermaston CND marches in the early Sixties to the final witness at the Peace Pentecost of 1986 at the Ministry of Defence base at Coulport on Loch Long where he was arrested for breech of the peace, chained with others, before the main gate at the base.

His last action was quite spontaneous, deciding suddenly to join the radical protest of praying in the Mouth of Evil and getting carried away as he said, by the sheer joy of witnessing to what he believed.

Roger was one of the most joyful members of the Iona Community. I remember like yesterday his passion for peace, his ferocious stammer, and his cheerful grin which to use a very non-pacifist phrase, had an affect on you like a 'petrol bomb'!

You weren't five minutes in his company before you were falling all over the place in helpless laughter.

He had a way of dealing with things — his stammer, for instance. He made it part of him but it was a real affliction to one so glad to communicate the urgent news of Peace on Earth.

There is a story of a well-known charismatic Christian having a conversation with Roger and the story goes:

Roger: 'Of course I speak in tongues myself.'

Charismatic: 'Really! How very interesting.'

Roger: Oh er yes, I often speak in tongues — of course it never was much use to me.'

Charismatic: (chastened) 'No?'

Roger: 'No, er you see, no-one could ever understand what I was saying anyway!'

But again, that is just a true story of the hilarious, Christian devotion of the man.

Like the story Albert MacAdam tells of Roger, having fallen two hundred feet in the Cuillins of Skye, singing his way through the hymn book with broken legs and a nightmare of frostbite ahead of him, saved as his ice axe caught on a promontory and finally rescued by the RAF Helicopter Service.

Said Mary at his funeral at which we sang Psalm 121: 'Roger would have had a good laugh at the verse "my foot he'll not let slide" — he fell two hundred feet and ended up in Raigmore Hospital.'

Going across in the ferry to Iona, Roger said to me: 'I'm going to recommend to you the second best book I have ever read — it's Gerry Hughes's: *The God of Surprises*. That really is the second best book I have read in my whole life outside the Bible.'

So I said, as was expected: 'What's the best book then?' 'Oh,' said Roger grinning, 'the *Fate of the Earth* — haven't I sent you a copy? Oh well, everyone knows that *Fate of the Earth* of course speaks of re-inventing politics and choosing between halting the arms race or becoming a republic of insects which are the only creatures to survive a nuclear holocaust.'

In view of Roger's recommendation I can feel that there is no more appropriate a way of ending this book than by quoting from his second favourite book *Fate of the Earth*, by Jonathan Schell.

In weighing the fate of the earth, and with it, our own fate, we stand before a mystery, and in tampering with the earth we tamper with a mystery. We are in deep ignorance. Our ignorance should dispose us to wonder, our wonder should make us humble, our humility should inspire us to reverence and caution, and our reverence and caution should lead us to act without delay to withdraw the threat we now pose to the earth and to ourselves.

CURRENT PUBLICATIONS OF THE IONA COMMUNITY

THE WHOLE EARTH SHALL CRY GLORY — Paperback ISBN 0 947988 00 9

THE WHOLE EARTH SHALL CRY GLORY — Hardback ISBN 0 947988 04 1
Iona prayers by Rev. George F. MacLeod

THE IONA COMMUNITY WORSHIP BOOK — ISBN 0 947988 28 9
Iona Community

THE CORACLE — REBUILDING THE COMMON LIFE — ISBN 0 947988 25 4
Jubilee reprint of Foundation Documents of the Iona Community

PEACE AND ADVENTURE — ISBN 0 9501351 6 X
Ellen Murray

90 RECIPES FROM THE IONA COMMUNITY — ISBN 0 947988 17 3
Sue Pattison

RE-INVENTING THEOLOGY — ISBN 0 947988 29 7
Ian M. Fraser

MEANING THE LORD'S PRAYER — ISBN 0 947988 30 0
George T. H. Reid

PARABLES AND PATTER — ISBN 0 947988 33 5
Erik Cramb

HEAVEN SHALL NOT WAIT (Wild Goose Songs Volume 1) — ISBN 0 947988 23 8
John Bell & Graham Maule

WILD GOOSE SONGS — VOLUME 2 — ISBN 0 947988 27 0
John Bell & Graham Maule

LOVE FROM BELOW (Wild Goose Songs Volume 3) — ISBN 0 947988 34 3
John Bell & Graham Maule

A TOUCHING PLACE — Cassette No.IC/WGP/004
Wild Goose Worship Group

CLOTH FOR THE CRADLE — Cassette No.IC/WGP/007
Wild Goose Worship Group

LOVE FROM BELOW — Cassette No.IC/WGP/008
Wild Goose Worship Group

FOLLY AND LOVE — Cassette No.IC/WGP/005
Iona Abbey

FREEDOM IS COMING — Cassette No.IC/WGP/006

FREEDOM IS COMING — ISBN 91 86788 15 7
Utryck

MANY AND GREAT (World Church Songs - Volume 1) — ISBN 0 947988 40 8
John Bell & Graham Maule

MANY AND GREAT — Cassette IC/WGP/009
Wild Goose Worship Group

WILD GOOSE PRINTS No.1 — ISBN 0 947988 06 8
John Bell & Graham Maule

WILD GOOSE PRINTS No.2 — ISBN 0 947988 10 6
John Bell & Graham Maule

WILD GOOSE PRINTS No.3 — ISBN 0 947988 24 6
John Bell & Graham Maule

WILD GOOSE PRINTS No.4 — ISBN 0 947988 35 1
John Bell & Graham Maule

WILD GOOSE PRINTS No. 5 — ISBN 0 947988 41 6
John Bell & Graham Maule

EH . . . JESUS . . . YES, PETER . . . ? Book 1 — ISBN 0 947988 20 3
John Bell & Graham Maule

EH . . . JESUS . . . YES, PETER . . .? Book 2 — ISBN 0 947988 31 9
John Bell & Graham Maule

WHAT IS THE IONA COMMUNITY? — ISBN 0 947988 07 6
Iona Community

CO-OPERATION VERSUS EXPLOITATION — ISBN 0 947988 22 X
Walter Fyfe

COLUMBA — ISBN 0 947988 11 4
Mitchell Bunting

FEEL IT — Detached Youth Work In Action — ISBN 0 947988 32 7
Cilla McKenna

PRAISING A MYSTERY — ISBN 0 947988 36 X
Brian Wren

BRING MANY NAMES — ISBN 0 947988 37 8
Brian Wren